Détente

Détente

Prospects for Democracy and Dictatorship

Aleksandr Solzhenitsyn

with commentary by
Arthur Schlesinger Jr.
Alex Simirenko
Melvin Gurtov
Lynn Turgeon
Amitai Etzioni
Richard Lowenthal
Norman Birnbaum
Irving Louis Horowitz

Transaction Books
New Brunswick (U.S.A.) and London (U.K.)

Library of Congress Catalog Number: 79-66443
ISBN: 0-87855-352-5 (cloth); 0-87855-750-4 (paper)
Printed in the United States of America

Library of Congress Cataloging in Publication Data

Solzhenitsyn, Aleksandr Isaevich, 1918-
  Détente.

(Issues in contemporary civilization)
1. Russia—Foreign relations—1935-1975.
2. Russia—Foreign relations—United States.
3. United States—Foreign relations—Russia.
4. Russia—Politics and government—1953-
5. Civilization, Modern—1950- 6. Solzhenitsyn, Aleksandr Isaevich, 1918- I. Schlesinger, Arthur Meier, 1917- II. Title.
DK274.S613 1979   327.47'073   79-66443

Contents

The Exhausted West

The split in today's world is perceptible even at a hasty glance. Any of our contemporaries readily identifies two world powers, each of them capable of entirely destroying the other. However, understanding of the split often is limited to this political conception, to the illusion that danger may be abolished through successful diplomatic negotiations or by achieving a balance of armed forces. The truth is that the split is a much profounder and a more alienating one, that the rifts are more than one can see at first glance. This deep manifold split bears the danger of manifold disaster for all of us, in accordance with the ancient truth that a Kingdom—in this case, our Earth—divided against itself cannot stand.

There is the concept of Third World: thus we have three worlds. Undoubtedly, however, the number is even greater; we are just too far away to see. Any ancient, deeply rooted autonomous culture, especially if it is spread over a wide part of the earth's surface, constitutes an autonomous world, full of riddles and surprises to Western thinking. At a minimum, we must include in this category China, India, the Muslim world, and Africa, if indeed we accept the approximation of viewing the last two as compact units. For one thousand years Russia belonged to such a category, although Western thinking systematically committed the mistake of denying its autonomous character and therefore never understood it, just as today the West does not understand Russia in Communist captivity. It may be that in the past years Japan has increasingly become a distant part of the West—I am no judge here; but as for Israel, for instance, it seems to me that it stands apart from the Western world, in that its state system is fundamentally linked to religion.

How short a time ago, relatively, the small, new European world was easily seizing colonies everywhere, not only without anticipating any real resistance but also usually despising any possible values in the conquered peoples' approach to life. On the face of it, it was an overwhelming success; there were no geographic frontiers to it. Western society expanded in a triumph of human independence and power. And all of a sudden in the twentieth century came the discovery of its fragility and friability. We now see that the conquests proved to be short-lived and precarious, and this in turn points to defects in the Western view of the world that led to these conquests. Relations with the former colonial world have now reversed: the Western world often goes to extremes of subservience. It is difficult yet to estimate the total size of the bill that former colonial countries will present to the West, and it is difficult to predict whether the surrender not only of its last colonies, but of everything it owns will be sufficient for the West to foot the bill.

But the blindness of superiority continues in spite of all and upholds the belief that vast regions everywhere on our planet should develop and mature to the level of present-day Western systems, which in theory are the best and in practice the most attractive. There is the belief that all those other worlds are being only temporarily prevented by wicked governments or by heavy crises or by their own barbarity and incomprehension from taking the way of Western pluralistic democracy and adopting the Western way of life; countries are judged on their progress in this direction. However, this is a conception that developed out of Western incomprehension of the essence of other worlds, out of the mistake of measuring them all with a Western yardstick. The real picture of our planet's development is quite different.

Anguish about our divided world gave birth to the theory of convergence between leading Western countries and the Soviet Union. It is a soothing theory, which overlooks the fact that these worlds are not at all developing into similarity; neither one can be transformed into the other without the use of violence. Besides, convergence inevitably means acceptance of the other side's defects, too, and this is hardly desirable.

If I were today addressing an audience in my country, examining the overall pattern of the world's rifts, I would concentrate on the East's calamities. But since my forced exile in the West has now lasted four years and since my audience is a Western one, I think it may be of greater interest to concentrate on certain aspects of the West in our day, such as I see them.

This may be the most striking feature that an outside observer notices in the West today. The Western world has lost its civil courage, both as a whole and separately, in each country, each government, each political party, and of course in the United Nations.

Such a decline in courage is particularly noticeable among the ruling groups and the intellectual elite, causing an impression of loss of courage by the entire society. Of course there are many courageous individuals, but they have no determining influence on public life. Political and intellectual bureaucrats show depression, passivity, and perplexity in their actions and in their statements, and even more so in theoretical reflections to explain how realistic, reasonable, as well as intellectually and even morally warranted it is to base state policies on weakness and cowardice. And decline in courage is ironically emphasized by occasional explosions of anger and inflexibility on the part of the same bureaucrats when dealing with weak governments and weak countries, not supported by anyone, or with currents that cannot offer any resistance. But they get tongue-tied and paralyzed when they deal with powerful governments and threatening forces, with aggressors and international terrorists.

Should one point out that from ancient times decline in courage has been considered the beginning of the end?

When the modern Western states were created, the following principle was proclaimed: governments are meant to serve man, and man lives to be free and to pursue happiness. (See, for example, the American Declaration of Independence.) Now at last, during past decades, technical and social progress have permitted the realization of such aspirations: the welfare state. Every citizen has been granted the desired freedom and material goods in such quantity and of such quality as to guarantee, in theory, the achievement of happiness, in the morally inferior sense that has come into being during those same decades. In the process, however, one psychological detail has been overlooked: the constant desire to have still more things and a still better life, and the struggle to obtain them imprints many Western faces with worry and even depression, though it is customary to conceal such feelings. Active and tense competition permeates all human thoughts without opening a way to free spiritual development. The individual's independence from many types of state pressure has been guaranteed; the majority of people have been granted well-being to an extent their fathers and grandfathers could not even dream about. It has become possible to raise young people according to these ideals, leading them to physical splendor, happiness, possession of material goods, money, and leisure, to an almost unlimited freedom of enjoyment. So who should now renounce all this, why and for what should one risk one's precious life in defense of common values, and particularly in such nebulous cases as when the security of one's nation must be defended in a distant country?

Even biology knows that habitual extreme safety and well-being are not advantageous for a living organism. Today, well-being in the life of Western society has begun to reveal its pernicious mask.

Western society has given itself the organization best

suited to its purposes, based, I would say, on the letter of
the law. The limits of human rights and righteousness are
determined by a system of laws; such limits are very
broad. People in the West have acquired considerable
skill in using, interpreting, and manipulating law. Any
conflict is solved according to the letter of the law, and this
is considered to be the supreme solution. If one is right
from a legal point of view, nothing more is required.
Nobody may mention that one could still not be entirely
right, and urge self-restraint, a willingness to renounce
such legal rights, sacrifice, and selfless risk: it would
sound simply absurd. One almost never sees voluntary
self-restraint. Everybody operates at the extreme limit of
those legal frames.

I have spent all my life under a Communist regime, and
I will tell you that a society without any objective legal
scale is a terrible one indeed. But a society with no other
scale but the legal one is not quite worthy of man either. A
society that is based on the letter of the law and never
reaches any higher is taking very small advantage of the
high level of human possibilities. The letter of the law is
too cold and formal to have a beneficial influence on
society. Whenever the tissue of life is woven of legalistic
relations, there is an atmosphere of moral mediocrity,
paralyzing man's noblest impulses.

And it will be, simply, impossible to stand through the
trials of this threatening century with only the support of a
legalistic structure.

In today's Western society, the inequality has been
revealed of freedom for good deeds and freedom for evil
deeds. A statesman who wants to achieve something
important and highly constructive for his country has to
move cautiously and even timidly: there are thousands of
hasty and irresponsible critics around him; parliament
and the press keep rebuffing him. As he moves ahead, he
has to prove that each single step of his is well founded and
absolutely flawless. In fact, an outstanding and particularly gifted person who has unusual and unexpected

initiatives in mind hardly gets a chance to assert himself; from the very beginning, dozens of traps will be set for him. Thus mediocrity triumphs, with the excuse of restrictions imposed by democracy.

It is feasible and easy everywhere to undermine administrative power, and, indeed, it has been drastically weakened in all Western countries. The defense of individual rights has reached such extremes as to make society as a whole defenseless against certain individuals. It is time, in the West, to defend not so much human rights as human obligations.

Destructive and irresponsible freedom has been granted boundless space. Society appears to have little defense against the abyss of human decadence, such as, for example, the misuse of liberty for moral violence against young people, motion pictures full of pornography, crime, and horror. It is considered to be part of freedom and theoretically counterbalanced by the young people's right not to look or not to accept. Life organized legalistically has thus shown its inability to defend itself against the corrosion of evil.

And what shall we say about criminality as such? Legal frames (especially in the United States) are broad enough to encourage not only individual freedom but also certain individual crimes. The culprit can go unpunished or obtain undeserved leniency with the support of thousands of public defenders. When a government starts an earnest fight against terrorism, public opinion immediately accuses it of violating the terrorists' civil rights. There are many such cases.

Such a tilt of freedom in the direction of evil has come about gradually, but it was evidently born primarily of a humanistic and benevolent concept according to which there is no evil inherent in human nature; the world belongs to mankind and all the defects of life are caused by wrong social systems, which must be corrected. Strangely enough, though the best social conditions have been achieved in the West, there still is criminality and there even is considerably more of it than in the pauper and lawless Soviet society.

The press too, of course, enjoys the widest freedom (I shall be using the word press to include all media). But what sort of use does it make of this freedom?

Here again, the main concern is not to infringe the letter of the law. There is no moral responsibility for deformation or disproportion. What sort of responsibility does a journalist have to his readers, or to history? If he has misled public opinion or the government by inaccurate information or wrong conclusions, do we know of any cases of public recognition and rectification of such mistakes by the same journalist or the same newspaper? No, it hardly ever happens, because it would damage sales. A nation may be the victim of such a mistake, but the journalist always gets away with it. One may safely assume that he will start writing the opposite with renewed self-assurance.

Because instant and credible information has to be given, it becomes necessary to resort to guesswork, rumors, and suppositions to fill in the voids, and none of them will ever be rectified; they will stay on in the readers' memory. How many hasty, immature, superficial, and misleading judgments are expressed every day, confusing readers, without any verification? The press can both simulate public opinion and miseducate it. Thus we may see terrorists made heroes, or secret matters pertaining to one's nation's defense publicly revealed, or we may witness shameless intrusion on the privacy of well-known people under the slogan "everyone is entitled to know everything." But this is a false slogan, characteristic of a false era: people also have the right not to know, and it is a much more valuable one. The right not to have their divine souls stuffed with gossip, nonsense, vain talk. A person who works and leads a meaningful life does not need this excessive burdening flow of information.

Hastiness and superficiality are the psychic disease of the twentieth century, and more than anywhere else this disease is reflected in the press.

Such as it is, however, the press has become the greatest power within the Western countries, more powerful than the legislature, the executive, and the judiciary. One would then like to ask: By what law has it been elected and to whom is it responsible? In the Communist East, a journalist is frankly appointed as a state official. But who has granted Western journalists their power, for how long a time, and with what prerogatives?

There is yet another surprise for someone coming from the East, where the press is rigorously unified: one gradually discovers a common trend of preferences within the Western press as a whole. It is a fashion; there are generally accepted patterns of judgment and there may be common corporate interests, the sum effect being not competition but unification. Enormous freedom exists for the press, but not the readership, because newspapers mostly give emphasis to those opinions that do not too openly contradict their own and the general trend.

Without any censorship, in the West, fashionable trends of thought are carefully separated from those that are not fashionable. Nothing is forbidden, but what is not fashionable will hardly ever find its way into periodicals or books or be heard in colleges. Legally, your researchers are free, but they are conditioned by the fashion of the day. There is no open violence such as in the East; however, a selection dictated by fashion and the need to match mass standards frequently prevents independent-minded people from giving their contribution to public life. There is a dangerous tendency to form a herd, shutting off successful development. I have received letters in America from highly intelligent persons, maybe a teacher in a faraway small college who could do much for the renewal and salvation of his country, but his country cannot hear him because the media are not interested in him. This gives birth to strong mass prejudices, to blindness, which is most dangerous in our dynamic era. There is, for instance, a self-deluding interpretation of the contemporary world situation. It works as a sort of petrified armor around people's minds. Human voices from seventeen countries of Eastern Europe and Eastern Asia cannot pierce it. It will be broken only by the pitiless crowbar of events.

I have mentioned a few traits of Western life that surprise and shock a new arrival to this world. The purpose and scope of this speech will not allow me to continue such a review, to look into the influence of these Western characteristics on important aspects of a nation's life, such as elementary education, or advanced education in the humanities and in art.

It is almost universally recognized that the West shows all the world a way to successful economic development, even though in the past years it has been strongly disturbed by chaotic inflation. However, many people living in the West are dissatisfied with their own society. They despise it or accuse it of not being up to the level of maturity attained by mankind. A number of such critics turn to socialism, which is a false and dangerous current.

I hope that no one present will suspect me of offering my personal criticism of the Western system to present socialism as an alternative. Having experienced applied socialism in a country where the alternative has been realized, I certainly will not speak for it. The well-known Soviet mathematician Shafarevich, a member of the Soviet Academy of Science, has written a brilliant book under the title *Socialism;* it is a profound analysis showing that socialism of any type and shade leads to a total destruction of the human spirit and to a leveling of mankind unto death. Shafarevich's book was published in France almost two years ago and so far no one has been found to refute it. It will shortly be published in English in the United States.

But should someone ask me whether I would indicate the West such as it is today as a model for my country, frankly I would have to answer negatively. No, I could not recommend your society in its present state as an ideal for the transformation of ours. Through intense suffering our country has now achieved a spiritual development of such intensity that the Western system in its present state of spiritual exhaustion does not look attractive. Even those characteristics of your life that I have just mentioned are extremely saddening.

A fact that cannot be disputed is the weakening of human beings in the West, while in the East they are becoming firmer and stronger. Six decades for our people and three decades for the people of Eastern Europe: during that time we have been through a spritual training far in advance of Western experience. Life's complexity and mortal weight have produced stronger, deeper, and more interesting characters than those generated by standardized Western well-being. Therefore, if our society were to be transformed into yours, it would mean an improvement in certain aspects, but also a change for the worse on some particularly significant scores. It is true, no doubt, that a society cannot remain in an abyss of lawlessness, as is the case in our country. But it is also demeaning for it to elect such mechanical legalistic smoothness as you have. After the suffering of decades of violence and oppression, the human soul longs for things higher, warmer, and purer than those offered by today's mass living habits, introduced by the revolting invasion of publicity, by TV stupor, and by intolerable music.

There are meaningful warnings that history gives a threatened or perishing society. They are, for instance, the decadence of art, or a lack of great statesmen. There are open and evident warnings, too. The center of your democracy and of your culture is left without electric power for a few hours only, and all of a sudden crowds of American citizens start looting and creating havoc. The smooth surface film must be very thin, then, the social system quite unstable and unhealthy.

But the fight for our planet, physical and spiritual, a fight of cosmic proportions, is not a vague matter of the future; it has already started. The forces of Evil have begun their offensive—you can feel their pressure—and yet your screens and publications are full of prescribed smiles and raised glasses. What is the joy about?

Very well known representatives of your society, such as George Kennan, say: we cannot apply moral criteria to politics. Thus we mix good and evil, right and wrong, and make space for the absolute triumph of absolute Evil in the world. On the contrary, only moral criteria can help the West against Communism's well-planned world strategy. There are no other criteria. Practical or occasional considerations of any kind will inevitably be swept away by strategy. After a certain level of the problem has been reached, legalistic thinking induces paralysis; it prevents one from seeing the size and meaning of events.

In spite of the abundance of information, or maybe because of it, the West has difficulties in understanding reality such as it is. There have been naive predictions by some American experts who believed that Angola would become the Soviet Union's Vietnam or that Cuban expeditions in Africa would best be stopped by special U.S. courtesy to Cuba. Kennan's advice to his own country—to begin unilateral disarmament—belongs to the same category. If you only knew how the youngest of the Kremlin officials laugh at your political wizards! As for Fidel Castro, he frankly scorns the United States, sending his troops to distant adventures from his country, right next to yours.

However, the most cruel mistake occurred with the failure to understand the Vietnam War. Some people sincerely wanted all wars to stop just as soon as possible; others believed that there should be room for national, or Communist, self-determination in Vietnam, or in Cambodia, as we see today with particular clarity. But members of the U.S. anti-war movement wound up being involved in the betrayal of Far Eastern nations, in a genocide and in the suffering today imposed on 30 million people there. Do those convinced pacifists hear the moans coming from there? Do they understand their responsibility today? Or do they prefer not to hear? The American intelligentsia lost its nerve, and as a consequence thereof danger has come much closer to the United States. But there is no awareness of this. Your short-sighted politicians who signed the hasty Vietnam capitulation seemingly gave America a carefree breathing spell; however, a hundredfold Vietnam now looms over you. That small Vietnam was a warning and an occasion to mobilize the nation's courage. But if a fullfledged America suffered a real defeat from a small, Communist half-country, how can the West hope to stand firm in the future?

I have previously had occasion to say that in the twentieth century Western democracy has not won any major war without help and protection from a powerful continental ally whose philosophy and ideology it did not question. In World War II against Hitler, instead of winning that war with its own forces, which would certainly have been sufficient, Western democracy cultivated another enemy, who would prove worse and more powerful yet, as Hitler never had so many resources and so many people, nor did he offer any attractive ideas, or have such a large number of supporters in the West as did the Soviet Union. At present, some Western voices have already spoken of obtaining protection from a third power against aggression in the next world conflict, if there is one; in this case, the shield would be China. But I would not wish such an outcome on any country in the world. First of all, it is again a doomed alliance with Evil; also, it would grant the United States a respite, but when at a later date China with its billion peopled turned around armed with American weapons, America itself would fall prey to a genocide similar to the one perpetrated in Cambodia in our day.

And yet—no weapons, no matter how powerful, can help the West until it overcomes its loss of will power. In a state of psychological weakness, weapons become a burden for the capitulating side. To defend oneself, one must also be ready to die; there is little such readiness in a society raised in the cult of material well-being. Nothing is left, then, but concessions, attempts to gain time and betrayal. Thus, at the shameful Belgrade Conference free Western diplomats in their weakness surrendered the line where enslaved members of Helsinki Watchgroups are sacrificing their lives.

Western thinking has become conservative: the world situation should stay as it is at any cost; there should be no changes. This debilitating dream of a status quo is the symptom of a society that has come to the end of its development. But one must be blind in order not to see that oceans no longer belong to the West, while land under its domination keeps shrinking. The two so-called world wars (they were not, by far, on a world scale, not yet) have meant the internal self-destruction of the small progressive West, which has thus prepared its own end. The next war (which does not have to be an atomic one and I do not believe it will be) may well bury Western civilization forever.

Facing such a danger, with such historical values in your past, at such a high level of realization of freedom, and apparently of devotion to freedom, how is it possible to lose to such an extent the will to defend oneself?

How has this unfavorable relation of forces come about? How did the West decline from its triumphal march to its present sickness? Have there been fatal turns and losses of direction in its development? It does not seem so. The West kept advancing socially in accordance with its proclaimed intentions, with the help of brilliant technological progress. And all of a sudden it found itself in its present state of weakness.

This means that the mistake must be at the root, at the very basis of human thinking in the past centuries. I refer to the prevailing Western view of the world, which was first born during the Renaissance and found its political expression in the period of the Enlightenment. It became the basis for government and social science and could be defined as rationalistic humanism or humanistic autonomy: the proclaimed and enforced autonomy of man from any higher force above him. It could also be called anthropocentricity, with man seen as the center of everything that exists.

The turn introduced by the Renaissance evidently was inevitable historically. The Middle Ages had come to a natural end by exhaustion, becoming an intolerable despotic repression of man's physical nature in favor of the spiritual one. Then, however, we turned our backs upon the Spirit and embraced all that is material with excessive and unwarranted zeal. This new way of thinking, which had imposed on us its guidance, did not admit the existence of intrinsic evil in man nor did it see any higher task than the attainment of happiness on earth. It based modern Western civilization on the dangerous trend to worship man and his material needs. Everything beyond physical well-being and accumulation of material goods, all other human requirements and characteristics of a subtler and higher nature, were left outside the area of attention of state and social systems, as if human life did not have any superior sense. That provided access for evil, of which in our day there is a free and constant flow. Mere freedom does not in the least solve all the problems of human life and it even adds a number of new ones.

However, in early democracies, as in American democracy at the time of its birth, all individual human rights were granted because man is God's creature. That is, freedom was given to the individual conditionally, in the assumption of his constant religious responsibility. Such was the heritage of the preceding thousand years. Two hundred, or even fifty, years ago, it would have seemed quite impossible, in America, that an individual could be granted boundless freedom simply for the satisfaction of his instincts or whims. Subsequently, however, all such limitations were discarded everywhere in the West; a total liberation occurred from the moral heritage of Christian centuries, with their great reserves of mercy and sacrifice. State systems were becoming increasingly and totally materialistic. The West ended up by truly enforcing human rights, sometimes even excessively, but man's sense of responsibility to God and society grew dimmer and dimmer. In the past decades, the legalistically selfish aspect of the Western approach and thinking has reached its final dimension, and the world wound up in a harsh spiritual crisis and a political impasse. All the glorified technological achievements of Progress, including the conquest of outer space, do not redeem the twentieth century's moral poverty, which no one could imagine even as late as in the nineteenth century.

As humanism in its development became more and more materialistic, it made itself increasingly accessible to speculation and manipulation, at first by socialism and then by communism. So that Karl Marx was able to say in 1884 that "communism is naturalized humanism."

This statement turned out to be not entirely senseless. One does see the same stones in the foundations of a de-spiritualized humanism and of any type of socialism: endless materialism; freedom from religion and religious responsibility, which under Communist regimes reaches the stage of anti-religious dictatorship; concentration on social structures, with a seemingly scientific approach. (This is typical of the Enlightenment in the eighteenth century and of Marxism.) Not by coincidence all of Communism's meaningless pledges and oaths are about Man, with a capital **M**, and his earthly happiness. At first glance it seems an ugly parallel: common traits in the thinking and way of life of today's West and today's East? But such is the logic of materialistic development.

The interrelationship is such, too, that the current of materialism that is most to the left always ends up by being stronger, more attractive, and victorious, because it is more consistent. Humanism without its Christian heritage cannot resist such competition. We watch this process in the past centuries and especially in the past decades, on a world scale as the situation becomes increasingly dramatic. Liberalism was inevitably displaced by radicalism, radicalism had to surrender to socialism, and socialism could never resist Communism. The Communist regime in the East could stand and grow thanks to the enthusiastic support it received from an enormous number of Western intellectuals who felt a kinship and refused to see Communism's crimes. When they no longer could ignore the crimes, they tried to justify them. In our Eastern countries, Communism has suffered a complete ideological defeat; it is zero and less than zero. But Western intellectuals still look at it with interest and with empathy, and this is precisely what makes it so immensely difficult for the West to withstand the East.

I am not examining here the case of a world-war disaster and the changes it would produce in society. As long as we wake up every morning under a peaceful sun, we have to lead an everyday life. There is a disaster, however, that has already been under way for quite some time. I am referring to the calamity of a despiritualized and irreligious humanistic consciousness.

Of such consciousness man is the touchstone, in judging everything on earth. Imperfect man, who is never free of pride, self-interest, envy, vanity, and dozens of other defects. We are now experiencing the consequences of mistakes that were not noticed at the beginning of the journey. On the way from the Renaissance to our day we have enriched our experience, but we have lost the concept of a Supreme Complete Entity, which used to restrain our passions and our irresponsibility. We have placed too much hope in political and social reforms, only to find that we were being deprived of our most precious possession: our spiritual life. In the East, it is destroyed by the dealings and machinations of the ruling party. In the West, commercial interests tend to suffocate it. This is the real crisis. The split in the world is less terrible than the similarity of the disease plaguing its main sections.

If humanism were right in declaring that man is born only to be happy, he would not be born to die. Since his body is doomed to die, his task on earth evidently must be of a more spiritual nature. It cannot be unrestrained enjoyment of everyday life. It cannot be the search for the best ways to obtain material goods and then cheerfully to get the most out of them. It has to be the fulfillment of a permanent, earnest duty, so that one's life journey may become an experience of moral growth, so that one may leave life a better human being than one started it. It is imperative to review the table of widespread human values. Its present incorrectness is astounding. It is not possible that assessment of the President's performance be reduced to the question of how much money one makes or of unlimited availability of gasoline. Only voluntary, inspired self-restraint can raise man above the world stream of materialism.

It would be retrogression to attach oneself today to the ossified formulas of the Enlightenment. Social dogmatism leaves us completely helpless before the trials of our times.

Even if we are spared destruction by war, our lives will have to change if we want to save life from self-destruction. We cannot avoid revising the fundamental definitions of human life and human society. Is it true that man is above everything? Is there no Superior Spirit above him? Is it right that man's life and society's activities have to be determined by material expansion in the first place? Is it permissible to promote such expansion to the detriment of our spiritual integrity?

If the world has not come to its end, it has approached a major turn in history, equal in importance to the turn from the Middle Ages to the Renaissance. It will exact from us a spiritual upsurge: we shall have to rise to a new height of vision, to a new level of life, where our physical nature will not be cursed as in the Middle Ages, but, even more important, our spiritual being will not be trampled upon as in the modern era.

This ascension will be similar to climbing up to the next anthropologic stage. No one on earth has any other way left but—upward.

'America: You Must Think About the World'

Most of those present here today are workers.
Creative workers. And I myself, having spent many
years of my life as a stone cutter, as a foundryman,
as a manual worker, in the name of all who have
shared this forced labor with me, like the two Gulag
prisoners whom you just saw, and on behalf of those
who are doing forced labor in our country, I can start
my speech today with the greeting: "Brothers!"
"Brothers in Labor."

And not to forget, also, the many honored guests
present here tonight, let me add: "Ladies and Gentlemen."

"Workers of the world unite!" Who of us has not
heard this slogan, which has been sounding through
the world for 125 years? Today you can find it in any
Soviet pamphlet as well as in every issue of Pravda.
But never have the leaders of the Communist revolution in the Soviet Union made application of these
words sincerely and in their full meaning. When many
lies have accumulated over the decades, we forget the
radical and basic lie which is not on the leaves of the
tree, but at its very roots.

Now, it's almost impossible to remember or to believe . . . For instance, I recently published—had
reprinted—a pamphlet from the year 1918. This was

*Address delivered in Washington, DC, on June 30, 1975. Sponsored by the
American Federation of Labor-Congress of Industrial Organizations
(AFL-CIO).*

a precise record of a meeting of all representatives of the Petrograd factories, that being the city known in our country as the "cradle of the Revolution."

I repeat, this was March 1918—only four months after the October Revolution—and all the representatives of the Petrograd factories were cursing the Communists, who had deceived them in all of their promises. What is more, not only had they abandoned Petrograd to cold and hunger, themselves having fled from Petrograd to Moscow, but had given orders to machinegun the crowds of workers in the courtyards of the factories who were demanding the election of independent factory committees.

Let me remind you, this was March 1918. Scarcely anyone now can recall the crushing of the Petrograd strikes in 1921, or the shooting of workers in Kolpino in the same year.

Among the leadership, the Central Committee of the Communist Party, at the beginning of the Revolution, all were emigre intellectuals who had returned, after the uprisings had already broken out in Russia, in order to carry through the Communist Revolution. One of them was a genuine worker, a highly skilled lathe operator until the last day of his life. This was Alexander Shliapnikov. Who knows that name today? Precisely because he expressed the true interests of the workers within the Communist leadership. In the years before the Revolution it was Shliapnikov who ran the whole Communist Party in Russia—not Lenin, who was an emigre. In 1921, he headed the Workers' Opposition which was charging the Communist leadership with betraying the workers' interests, with crushing and oppressing the proletariat and transforming itself into a bureaucracy.

Shliapnikov disappeared from sight. He was arrested somewhat later and since he firmly stood his ground he was shot in prison and his name is perhaps unknown to most people here today. But I remind you: before the Revolution the head of the Communist Party of Russia was Shliapnikov—not Lenin.

Since that time, the working class has never been able to stand up for its rights, and in distinction from all the western countries our working class only receives what they hand out to it. It only gets handouts. It cannot defend its simplest, everyday interests, and the least strike for pay or for better living conditions is viewed as counter-revolutionary. Thanks to the closed nature of the Soviet system, you have probably never heard of the textile strikes in 1930 in Ivanovo, or of the 1961 worker unrest in Murom and Alexandrovo, or of the major workers' uprising in Novocherkassk in 1962—this in the time of Khrushchev, after the thaw.

This story will shortly be published in detail in your country in Gulag Archipelago, volume 3. It is a story of how workers went in a peaceful demonstration to the Party City Committee, carrying portraits of Lenin, to request a change in economic conditions. They fired at them with machine guns and dispersed the crowds with tanks. No family dared even to collect its wounded and dead, but all were taken away in secret by the authorities.

Precisely to those present here I don't have to explain that in our country, since the Revolution, there's never been such a thing as a free trade union.

The leaders of the British trade unions are free to play the unworthy game of visiting Russia's so-called trade unions and receiving visits in return. But the AFL-CIO has never given in to these illusions.

The American workers' movement has never allowed itself to be blinded and to mistake slavery for freedom. And I, today, on behalf of all of our oppressed people, thank you for this!

When liberal thinkers and wise men of the West, who had forgotten the meaning of the word "liberty," were swearing that in the Soviet Union there were no concentration camps at all, the American Federation of Labor, published in 1947, a map of our concentration camps, and on behalf of all of the prisoners of those times, I want to thank the American workers' movement for this.

But just as we feel ourselves your allies here, there also exists another alliance—at first glance a strange one, a surprising one—but if you think about it, in fact, one which is well-grounded and easy to understand: this is the alliance between our Communist leaders and your capitalists.

This alliance is not new. The very famous Armand Hammer, who is flourishing here today, laid the basis for this when he made the first exploratory trip into Russia, still in Lenin's time, in the very first years of the Revolution. He was extremely successful in this intelligence mission and since that time for all these 50 years, we observe continuous and steady support by the businessmen of the West of the Soviet Communist leaders.

Their clumsy and awkward economy, which could never overcome its own difficulties by itself, is continually getting material and technological assistance. The major construction projects in the initial five-year plan were built exclusively with American technology and materials. Even Stalin recognized that two-thirds of what was needed was obtained from the West. And if today the Soviet Union has powerful military and police forces—in a country which is by contemporary standards poor—they are used to crush

our movement for freedóm in the Soviet Union—and
we have western capital to thank for this also.

Let me remind you of a recent incident which some
of you may have seen in the newspapers, although
others might have missed it: Certain of your businessmen, on their own initiative, established an exhibition
of criminological technology in Moscow. This was the
most recent and elaborate technology, which here, in
your country, is used to catch criminals, to bug them,
to spy on them, to photograph them, to tail them, to
identify criminals. This was taken to Moscow to an
exhibition in order that the Soviet KGB agents could
study it, as if not understanding what sort of criminals,
who would be hunted by the KGB.

The Soviet government was extremely interested in
this technology, and decided to purchase it. And your
businessmen were quite willing to sell it. Only when a
few sober voices here raised an uproar against it was
this deal blocked. Only for this reason it didn't take
place. But you have to realize how clever the KGB
is. This technology didn't have to stay two or three
weeks in a Soviet building under Soviet guard. Two
or three nights were enough for the KGB there to look
through it and copy it. And if today, persons are being
hunted down by the best and most advanced technology, for this, I can also thank your western capitalists.

This is something which is almost incomprehensible
to the human mind: that burning greed for profit
which goes beyond all reason, all self-control, all
conscience, only to get money.

I must say that Lenin foretold this whole process.
Lenin, who spent most of his life in the West and not
in Russia, who knew the West much better than Russia, always wrote and said that the western capitalists

would do anything to strengthen the economy of the USSR. They will compete with each other to sell us goods cheaper and sell them quicker, so that the Soviets will buy from one rather than from the other. He said: They will bring it themselves without thinking about their future. And, in a difficult moment, at a party meeting in Moscow, he said: "Comrades, don't panic, when things go very hard for us, we will give a rope to the bourgeoisie, and the bourgeoisie will hang itself."

Then, Karl Radek, whom you may have heard of, who was a very resourceful wit, said: "Vladimir Ilyich, but where are we going to get enough rope to hang the whole bourgeoisie?"

Lenin effortlessly replied, "They'll supply us with it."

Through the decades of the 1920s, the 1930s, the 1940s, the 1950s, the whole Soviet press wrote: Western capitalism, your end is near.

But it was as if the capitalists had not heard, could not understand, could not believe this.

Nikita Khrushchev came here and said, "We will bury you!" They didn't believe that, either. They took it as a joke.

Now, of course, they have become more clever in our country. Now they don't say "we are going to bury you" anymore, now they say "detente."

Nothing has changed in Communist ideology. The goals are the same as they were, but instead of the artless Khrushchev, who couldn't hold his tongue, now they say "detente."

In order to understand this, I will take the liberty of making a short historic survey—the history of such relations, which in different periods have been called "trade," "stabilization of the situation," "recognition of realities," and now "detente." These relations now are at least 40 years old.

Let me remind you with what sort of system they started.

The system was installed by armed uprising.

It dispersed the Constituent Assembly.

It capitulated to Germany—the common enemy.

It introduced execution without trial.

It crushed workers' strikes.

It plundered the villagers to such an unbelievable extent that the peasants revolted, and when this happened it crushed the peasants in the bloodiest possible way.

It shattered the Church.

It reduced 20 provinces of our country to a condition of famine.

This was in 1921, the famous Volga famine. A very typical Communist technique: To seize power without thinking of the fact that the productive forces will collapse, that the fields will not be sown, the factories will stop, that the country will decline into poverty and famine—but when poverty and hunger come, then they request the humanitarian world to help them. We see this in North Vietnam today, perhaps Portugal is approaching this also. And the same thing happened in Russia in 1921. When the three-year civil war, started by the Communists—and "civil war" was a slogan of the Communists, civil war was Lenin's purpose; read Lenin, this was his aim and his slogan—when they had ruined Russia by this civil war, then they asked America, "America, feed our hungry." And indeed, generous and magnanimous America did feed our hungry.

The so-called American Relief Administration was set up, headed by your future President Hoover, and indeed many millions of Russian lives were saved by this organization of yours.

But what sort of gratitude did you receive for this? In the USSR not only did they try to erase this whole event from the popular memory—it's almost impossible today in the Soviet press to find any reference to the American Relief Administration—but they even denounce it as a clever spy organization, a clever scheme of American imperialism to set up a spy network in Russia. I repeat, it was a system that introduced concentration camps for the first time in the history of the world.

A system that, in the 20th Century, was the first to introduce the use of hostages, that is to say, not to seize the person whom they were seeking, but rather a member, of his family or someone at random, and shoot that person.

This system of hostages and persecution of the family exists to this day. It is still the most powerful weapon of persecution, because the bravest person, who is not afraid for himself, still shivers at the threat to his family.

It is a system which was the first—long before Hitler—to employ false registration, that is, to say: "Such and such people have to come in to register." People would comply and then they were taken away to be annihilated.

We didn't have gas chambers in those days. We used barges. A hundred or a thousand persons were put into a barge and then it was sunk.

It was a system which deceived the workers in all of its decrees—the decree on land, the decree on peace, the decree on factories, the decree on freedom of the press.

It was a system which exterminated all additional parties, and let me make it clear to you that it not only disbanded the party itself, but destroyed its members. All members of every other party were exterminated. It was a system which carried out genocide of the peasantry; 15 million peasants were sent off to extermination.

It was a system which introduced serfdom, the so-called "passport system."

It was a system which, in time of peace, artificially created a famine, causing 6 million persons to die in the Ukraine in 1932 and 1933. They died on the very edge of Europe. And Europe didn't even notice it. The world didn't even notice it—6 million persons!

I could keep on enumerating these endlessly, but I have to stop because I have come to the year 1933 when, with all I have enumerated behind us, your President Roosevelt and your Congress recognized this system as one worthy of diplomatic recognition, of friendship and of assistance.

Let me remind you that the great Washington did not agree to recognize the French Convention because of its savagery. Let me remind you that in 1933, voices were raised in your country objecting to recognition of the Soviet Union. However, the recognition took place and this was the beginning of friendship and ultimately of a military alliance.

Let us remember that in 1904, the American press was delighted at the Japanese victories and everyone wanted Russia's defeat because it was a conservative country. I want to remind you that in 1914 reproaches were directed at France and England for having entered into an alliance with such a conservative country as Russia.

The scope and the direction of my speech today do not permit me to say more about pre-revolutionary Russia. I will just say that information about pre-revolutionary Russia was obtained by the West from persons who were either not sufficiently competent or not sufficiently conscientious. I will just cite for the sake of comparison a number of figures which you can read for yourself in Gulag Archipelago, volume 1, which has been published in the United States, and perhaps many of you may have read it. These are the figures:

According to calculations by specialists, based on the most precise objective statistics, in pre-revolutionary Russia, during the 80 years before the revolution —years of the revolutionary movement when there were attempts on the Tsar's life, assassination of a Tsar, revolution—during these years about 17 persons a year were executed. The famous Spanish Inquisition, during the decades when it was at the height of its persecution, destroyed perhaps 10 persons a month. In the Archipelago—I cite a book which was published by the Cheka in 1920, proudly reporting on its revolutionary work in 1918 and 1919 and apologizing that its data were not quite complete—in 1918 and 1919 the Cheka executed, without trial, more than a thousand persons a month! This was written by the Cheka itself, before it understood how this would look to history.

At the height of Stalin's terror in 1937-38, if we divide the number of persons executed by the number of months, we get more than 40,000 persons shot per month! Here are the figures: 17 a year, 10 a month, more than 1,000 a month, more than 40,000 a month! Thus, that which had made it difficult for the democratic West to form an alliance with pre-revolutionary Russia had, by 1941, grown to such an extent and still did not prevent the entire united democracy of the world—England, France, the United States, Canada, Australia and small countries—from entering into a military alliance with the Soviet Union. How is this to be explained? How can we understand it? Here we can offer a few explanations. The first, I think, is that the entire united democracy of the world was too weak to fight against Hitler's Germany alone. If this is the case, then it is a terrible sign. It is a terrible portent for the present day. If all these countries together could not defeat Hitler's little Germany, what are they going to do today, when more than half the globe is flooded with totalitarianism? I don't want to accept this explanation.

The second explanation is perhaps that there was simply an attack of panic—of fear—among the statesmen of the day. They simply didn't have sufficient confidence in themselves, they simply had no strength of spirit, and in this confused state decided to enter into an alliance with Soviet totalitarianism. This is also not flattering to the West.

Finally, the third explanation is that it was a deliberate device. Democracy did not want to defend itself. For defense it wanted to use another totalitarian system, the Soviet totalitarian system.

I'm not talking now about the moral evaluation of this, I'm going to talk about that later. But in terms of simple calculation, how shortsighted, what profound self-deception!

We have a Russian proverb: "Do not call a wolf to help you against the dogs." If dogs are attacking and tearing at you, fight against the dogs, but do not call a wolf for help. Because when the wolves come, they will destroy the dogs, but they will also tear you apart.

World democracy could have defeated one totalitarian regime after another, the German, then the Soviet. Instead, it strengthened Soviet totalitarianism, helped bring into existence a third totalitarianism, that of China, and all this finally precipitated the present world situation.

Roosevelt, in Teheran, during one of his last toasts, said the following: "I do not doubt that the three of us"—meaning Roosevelt, Churchill and Stalin—"lead our peoples in accordance with their desires, in accordance with their aims." How are we to explain this? Let the historians worry about that. At the time, we listened and were astonished. We thought, "when we reach Europe, we will meet the Americans, and we will tell them." I was among the troops that were marching towards the Elbe. A little bit more and I would have reached the Elbe and would have shaken the hands of your American soldiers. But just before that happened, I was taken off to prison and my meeting did not take place.

But now, after all this great delay, the same hand has thrown me out of the country and here I am, instead of the meeting at the Elbe. After a delay of 30 years, my Elbe is here today. I am here to tell you, as a friend of the United States, what, as friends, we wanted to tell you then, but which our soldiers were prevented from telling you on the Elbe.

There is another Russian proverb: "The yes-man is your enemy, but your friend will argue with you." It is precisely because I am the friend of the United States, precisely because my speech is prompted by friendship, that I have come to tell you: "My friends, I'm not going to tell you sweet words. The situation in the world is not just dangerous, it isn't just threatening, it is catastrophic."

Something that is incomprehensible to the ordinary human mind has taken place. We over there, the powerless, average Soviet people, couldn't understand, year after year and decade after decade, what was happening. How were we to explain this? England, France, the United States, were victorious in World War II. Victorious states always dictate peace; they receive firm conditions; they create the sort of situation which accords with their philosophy, their concept of liberty, their concept of national interest.

Instead of this, beginning in Yalta, your statesmen of the West, for some inexplicable reason, have signed one capitulation after another. Never did the West or your President Roosevelt impose any conditions on the Soviet Union for obtaining aid. He gave unlimited aid, and then unlimited concessions. Already in Yalta, without any necessity, the occupation of Mongolia, Moldavia, Estonia, Latvia, Lithuania was silently recognized. Immediately after that, almost nothing was done to protect eastern Europe, and seven or eight more countries were surrendered.

Stalin demanded that the Soviet citizens who did not want to return home be handed over to him, and the western countries handed over 1.5 million human beings. How was this done? They took them by force. English soldiers killed Russians who did not want to become prisoners of Stalin, and drove them by force to Stalin to be exterminated. This has recently come to light—just a few years ago—a million and a half human beings. How could the Western democracies have done this?

And after that, for another 30 years, the constant retreat, the surrender of one country after another, to such a point that there are Soviet satellites even in Africa; almost all of Asia is taken over by them; Portugal is rolling down the precipice.

During those 30 years, more was surrendered to totalitarianism than any defeated country has ever surrendered after any war in history. There was no war, but there might as well have been.

For a long time we in the East couldn't understand this. We couldn't understand the flabbiness of the truce concluded in Vietnam. Any average Soviet citizen understood that this was a sly device which made it possible for North Vietnam to take over South Vietnam when it so chose. And suddenly, this was rewarded by the Nobel Prize for Peace—a tragic and ironic prize.

A very dangerous state of mind can arise as a result of this 30 years of retreat: give in as quickly as possible, give up as quickly as possible, peace and quiet at any cost.

This is what many western papers wrote: "Let's hurry up an end the bloodshed in Vietnam and have national unity there." But at the Berlin Wall no one talked of national unity. One of your leading newspapers, after the end of Vietnam, had a full headline: "The Blessed Silence." I would not wish that kind of "blessed silence" on my worst enemy. I would not wish that kind of national unity on my worst enemy.

I spent 11 years in the Archipelago, and for half of my lifetime I have studied this question. Looking at this terrible tragedy in Vietnam from a distance, I can tell you, a million persons will be simply exterminated, while 4 to 5 million (in accordance with the scale of Vietnam) will find themselves in concentration camps and will be rebuilding Vietnam. And what is happening in Cambodia you already know. It is genocide. It is full and complete destruction but in a new form. Once again their technology is not up to building gas chambers. So, in a few hours, the entire capital city—the guilty capital city—is emptied out: old people, women, children are driven out without belongings, without food. "Go and die!"

This is very dangerous for one's view of the world when this feeling comes on: "Go ahead, give it up."

We already hear voices in your country and in the West—"Give up Korea and we will live quietly. Give up Portugal, of course; give up Japan, give up Israel, give up Taiwan, the Philippines, Malaysia, Thailand, give up 10 more African countries. Just let us live in peace and quiet. Just let us drive our big cars on our splendid highways; just let us play tennis and golf, in peace and quiet; just let us mix our cocktails in peace and quiet as we are accustomed to doing; just let us see the beautiful toothy smile with a glass in hand on every advertisement page of our magazines."

But look how things have turned out: Now in the West this has all turned into an accusation against the United States. Now, in the West, we hear very many voices saying, "It's your fault, America." And, here, I must decisively defend the United States against these accusations.

I have to say that the United States, of all the countries of the West, is the least guilty in all this and has done the most in order to prevent it. The United States has helped Europe to win the First and the Second World Wars. It twice raised Europe from post-war destruction—twice—for 10, 20, 30 years it has stood as a shield protecting Europe while European countries were counting their nickels, to avoid paying for their armies (better yet to have none at all) to avoid paying for armaments, thinking about how to leave NATO, knowing that in any case America will protect them anyway. These countries started it all, despite their thousands of years of civilization and culture, even though they are closer and should have known better.

I came to your continent—for two months I have been travelling in its wide open spaces and I agree: here you do not feel the nearness of it all, the immediacy of it all. And here it is possible to miscalculate. Here you must make a spiritual effort to understand the acuteness of the world situation. The United States of America has long shown itself to be the most magnanimous, the most generous country in the world. Wherever there is a flood, an earthquake, a fire, a natural disaster, disease, who is the first to help? The United States. Who helps the most and unselfishly? The United States.

And what do we hear in reply? Reproaches, curses, "Yankee Go Home." American cultural centers are burned, and the representatives of the Third World jump on tables to vote against the United States.

But this does not take the load off America's shoulders. The course of history—whether you like it or not —has made you the leaders of the world. Your country can no longer think provincially. Your political leaders can no longer think only of their own states, of their parties, of petty arrangements which may or may not lead to promotion. You must think about the whole world, and when the new political crisis in the world will arise (I think we have just come to the end of a very acute crisis and the next one will come any moment) the main decisions will fall anyway on the shoulders of the United States of America.

And while already here, I have heard some explanations of the situation. Let me quote some of them: "It is impossible to protect those who do not have the will to defend themselves." I agree with that, but this was said about South Vietnam. In one-half of today's Europe and in three-quarters of today's world the will to defend oneself is even less than it was in South Vietnam.

We are told: "We cannot defend those who are unable to defend themselves with their own human resources." But against the overwhilming powers of totalitarianism, when all of this power is thrown against a country—no country can defend itself with its own resources. For instance, Japan doesn't have a standing army.

We are told, "We should not protect those who do not have full democracy." This is the most remarkable argument of the lot. This is the Leitmotif I hear in your newspapers and in the speeches of some of your political leaders. Who in the world, ever, on the front line of defense against totalitarianism has been able to sustain full democracy? You, the united democracies of the world, were not able to sustain it. America, England, France, Canada, Australia together did not sustain it. At the first threat of Hitlerism, you stretched out your hands to Stalin. You call that sustaining democracy?

And there is more of the same (there were many of these speeches in a row): "If the Soviet Union is going to use detente for its own ends, then we. . . ." But what will happen then? The Soviet Union has used detente in its own interests, is using it now and will continue to use it in its own interests! For example, China and the Soviet Union, both actively participating in detente, have quietly grabbed three countries of Indochina. True, perhaps as a consolation, China will send you a ping-pong team. And just as the Soviet Union once sent you the pilots who once crossed the North Pole, in a few days you're flying into space together.

A typical diversion. I remember very well the year, this was June of 1937, when Chkalov, Baidukov and Beliakov heroically flew over the North Pole and landed in the state of Washington. This was the very year when Stalin was executing more than 40,000 persons a month. And Stalin knew what he was doing.

He sent those pilots and aroused in you a naive delight—the friendship of two countries across the North Pole. The pilots were heroic, nobody will say anything against them. But this was a show—a show to divert you from the real events of 1937. And what is the occasion now? Is it an anniversary—38 years? Is 38 years some kind of an anniversary? No, it is simply necessary to cover up Vietnam. And, once again, those pilots were sent here. The Chkalov Memorial was unveiled in the State of Washington. Chkalov was a hero and is worthy of a memorial. But, to present the true picture, behind the memorial there should have been a wall and on it there should have been a bas relief showing the executions, showing the skulls and bones.

We are also told (I apologize for so many quotes, but there are many more in your press and radio): "We cannot ignore the fact that North Vietnam and the Khmer Rouge have violated the agreement, but we're ready to look into the future." What does that mean? It means: let them exterminate people. But if these murderers, who live by violence, these executioners, offer us detente we will be happy to go along with them. As Willy Brandt once said: "I would even be willing to have detente with Stalin." At a time when Stalin was executing 40,000 a month, he would have been willing to have detente with Stalin?

Look into the future. This is how they looked into the future in 1933 and 1941, but it was a shortsighted look into the future. This is how they looked into the future two years ago when a senseless, incomprehensible, non-guaranteed truce in Vietnam was arranged, and it was a shortsighted view. There was such a hurry to make this truce that they forgot to liberate your own Americans from captivity. They were in such a hurry to sign this document that some

1,300 Americans, "Well, they have vanished; we can get by without them." How is that done? How can this be? Part of them, indeed, can be missing in action, but the leaders of North Vietnam themselves have admitted that some of them are still being kept in prison. And do they give you back your countrymen? No, they are not giving them back, and they are always raising new conditions. At first they said, "Remove Thieu from power." Now, they say, "Have the United States restore Vietnam, otherwise it's very difficult for us to find these people."

If the government of North Vietnam has difficulty explaining to you what happened with your brothers, with your American POWs who have not yet returned, I, on the basis of my experience in the Archipelago, can explain this quite clearly. There is a law in the Archipelago that those who have been treated the most harshly and who have withstood the most bravely, the most honest, the most courageous, the most unbending, never again come out into the world. They are never again shown to the world because they will tell such tales as the human mind cannot accept. A part of your returned POWs told you that they were tortured. This means that those who have remained were tortured even more, but did not yield an inch. These are your best people. These are your first heroes, who, in a solitary combat, have stood the test. And today, unfortunately, they cannot take courage from our applause. They can't hear it from their solitary cells where they may either die or sit 30 years, like Raoul Wallenberg, the Swedish diplomat who was seized in 1945 in the Soviet Union. He has been imprisoned for 30 years and they will not yield him up.

And you have some hysterical public figure who said: "I will go to North Vietnam. I will stand on my

knees and beg them to release our prisoners of war."
This isn't a political act—this is masochism.

To understand properly what detente has meant all
these 40 years—friendships, stabilization of the situation, trade, etc. I would have to tell you something,
which you have never seen or heard, of how it looked
from the other side. Let me tell you how it looked.
Mere acquaintance with an American, and God forbid that you should sit with him in a cafe or restaurant,
meant a 10-year term for suspicion of espionage.

In the first volume of Archipelago I tell of an event
which was not told me by some arrested person, but
by all of the members of the Supreme Court of the
USSR during those short days when I was in the
limelight under Khrushchev. One Soviet citizen was
in the United States and on his return said that in
the United States they have wonderful automobile
roads. The KGB arrested him and demanded a term
of 10 years. But the judge said: "I don't object, but
there is not enough evidence. Couldn't you find something else against him?" So the judge was exiled to
Sakhalin because he dared to argue and they gave
the other man 10 years. Can you imagine what a lie
he told? And what sort of praise this was of American
imperialism—in America there are good roads? Ten
years.

In 1945-46 through our prison cells passed a lot
of persons—and these were not ones who were coop-
erating with Hitler, although there were some of those,
too. These were not guilty of anything, but rather
persons who had just been in the West and had been
liberated from German prison camps by the Americans. This was considered a criminal act: liberated
by the Americans. That means he has seen the good
life. If he comes back he will talk about it. The most
terrible thing is not what he did but what he would

talk about. And all such persons got 10-year terms.

During Nixon's last visit to Moscow your American correspondents were reporting in the western way from the streets of Moscow. I am going down a Russian street with a microphone and asking the ordinary Soviet citizen: "Tell me please, what do you think about the meeting between Nixon and Brezhnev?" And, amazingly, every last person answered: "Wonderful. I'm delighted. I'm absolutely overjoyed!"

What does this mean? If I'm going down a street in Moscow and some American comes up to me with a microphone and asks me something, then I know that on the other side of him is a member of the state security, also with a microphone who is recording everything I say. You think that I'm going to say something that is going to put me in prison immediately? Of course I say: "It's wonderful; I'm overjoyed."

But what is the value of such correspondents if they simply transfer western techniques over there without thinking things through?

You helped us for many years with Lend Lease, but we've now done everything to forget this, to erase it from our minds, not to remember it if at all possible. And now, before I came into this hall, I delayed my visit to Washington a little in order to first take a look at some ordinary parts of America, going to various states and simply talking with people. I was told, and I learned this for the first time, that in every state during the war years there were Soviet-American friendship societies which collected assistance for Soviet people—warm clothes, canned food, gifts and sent them to the Soviet Union. But we not only never saw these; we not only never received them (they were distributed somewhere among the privileged circles) no one ever even told us that this was being done. I only learned about it for the first time here, this month, in the United States.

Everything poisonous which could be said about the United States was said in Stalin's days. And all of this is a heavy sediment which can be stirred up anytime. Any day the newspapers can come out with the headlines: "Bloodthirsty American imperialism wants to seize control of the world," and this poison will rise up from the sediment and many people in our country will believe this, and will be poisoned by it, and will consider you as aggressors. This is how detente has been managed on our side.

The Soviet system is so closed that it is almost impossible for you to understand from here. Your theoreticians and scholars write works trying to understand and explain how things occur there. Here are some naive explanations which are simply funny to Soviet citizens. Some say that the Soviet leaders have now given up their inhumane ideology. Not at all. They haven't given it up one bit.

Some say that in the Kremlin there are some on the left, some on the right. And they are fighting with each other, and we've got to behave in such a way as not to interfere with those on the left side. This is all fantasy: left . . . right. There is some sort of a struggle for power, but they all agree on the essentials.

There also exists the following theory, that now, thanks to the growth of technology, there is a technocracy in the Soviet Union, a growing number of engineers and the engineers are now running the economy and will soon determine the fate of the country, rather than the party. I will tell you, though, that the engineers determine the fate of the economy just as much as our generals determine the fate of the Army. That means zero. Everything is done the way the party demands. That's our system. Judge it for yourself.

It's a system where for 40 years there haven't been genuine elections but simply a comedy, a farce. Thus a system which has no legislative organs. It's a system without an independent press; a system without an independent judiciary; where the people have no influence either on external or internal policy; where any thought which is different from what the state thinks is crushed.

And let me tell you that electronic bugging in our country is such a simple thing that it's a matter of everyday life. You had an instance in the United States where a bugging caused an uproar which lasted for a year and a half. For us it's an everyday matter. Almost every apartment, every institution has got its bug and it doesn't surprise us in the least—we are used to it.

It's a system where unmasked butchers of millions like Molotov and others smaller than him have never been tried in the courts but retire on tremendous pensions in the greatest comfort. It's a system where the show still goes on today and to which every foreigner is introduced surrounded by a couple of planted agents working according to a set scenario. It's a system where the very constitution has never been carried out for one single day; where all the decisions mature in secrecy, high up in a small irresponsible group and then are released on us and on you like a bolt of lightning.

And what are the signatures of such persons worth? How could one rely on their signatures to documents of detente? You yourselves might ask your specialists now and they'll tell you that precisely in recent years the Soviet Union has succeeded in creating wonderful chemical weapons, missiles, which are even better than those used by the United States.

So what are we to conclude from that? Is detente needed or not? Not only is it needed, it's as necessary as air. It's the only way of saving the earth—instead of a world war to have detente, but a true detente, and if it has already been ruined by the bad word which we use for it—"detente"—then we should find another word for it.

I would say that there are very few, only three, main characteristics of such a true detente.

In the first place, there would be disarmament—not only disarmament from the use of war but also from the use of violence. We must stop using not only the sort of arms which are used to destroy one's neighbors, but the sort of arms which are used to oppress one's fellow countrymen. It is not detente if we here with you today can spend our time agreeably while over there people are groaning and dying and in psychiatric hospitals. Doctors are making their evening rounds, for the third time injecting people with drugs which destroy their brain cells.

The second sign of detente, I would say, is the following: that it be not one based on smiles, not on verbal concessions, but it has to be based on a firm foundation. You know the words from the Bible: "Build not on sand, but on rock." There has to be a guarantee that this will not be broken overnight and for this the other side—the other party to the agreement—must have its acts subject to public opinion, to the press, and to a freely elected parliament. And until such control exists there is absolutely no guarantee.

The third simple condition—what sort of detente is it when they employ the sort of inhumane propaganda which is proudly called in the Soviet Union "ideologi-

cal warfare." Let us not have that. If we're going to
be friends, let's be friends, if we're going to have detente, then let's have detente, and an end to ideological warfare.

The Soviet Union and the Communist countries can
conduct negotiations. They know how to do this. For
a long time they don't make any concessions and then
they give in a little bit. Then everyone says triumph-
antly, "Look, they've made a concession; it's time to
sign." The European negotiators of the 35 countries
for two years now have painfully been negotiating and
their nerves were stretched to the breaking point and
they finally gave in. A few women from the Communist countries can now marry foreigners. And a few
newspapermen are now going to be permitted to travel
a little more than before. They give 1/1,000th of
what natural law should provide. Matters which people should be able to do even before such negotiations are undertaken. And already there is joy. And
here in the West we hear many voices, saying: "Look,
they're making concessions; it's time to sign."

During these two years of negotiations, in all the
countries of eastern Europe, the pressure has increased, the oppression intensified, even in Yugoslavia
and Romania, leaving aside the other countries. And
it is precisely now that the Austrian chancellor says,
"We've got to sign this agreement as rapidly as
possible."

What sort of an agreement would this be? The
proposed agreement is the funeral of eastern Europe.
It means that western Europe would finally, once and
for all, sign away eastern Europe, stating that it is
perfectly willing to see eastern Europe be crushed
and overwhelmed once and for all, but please don't
bother us. And the Austrian chancellor thinks that
if all these countries are pushed into a mass grave,

Austria at the very edge of this grave will survive and not fall into it also.

And we, from our lives there, have concluded that violence can only be withstood by firmness.

You have to understand the nature of communism. The very ideology of communism, all of Lenin's teachings, are that anyone is considered to be a fool who doesn't take what's lying in front of him. If you can take it, take it. If you can attack, attack. But if there's a wall, then go back. And the Communist leaders respect only firmness and have contempt and laugh at persons who continually give in to them. Your people are now saying—and this is the last quotation I am going to give you from the statements of your leaders—"Power, without any attempt at conciliation, will lead to a world conflict." But I would say that power with continual subservience is no power at all.

But from our experience I can tell you that only firmness will make it possible to withstand the assaults of Communist totalitarianism. We see many historic examples, and let me give you some of them. Look at little Finland in 1939, which by its own forces withstood the attack. You, in 1948, defended Berlin only by your firmness of spirit, and there was no world conflict. In Korea in 1950 you stood up against the Communists, only by your firmness, and there was no world conflict. In 1962 you compelled the rockets to be removed from Cuba. Again it was only firmness, and there was no world conflict. And the late Konrad Adenauer conducted firm negotiations with Khrushchev and thus started a genuine detente with Khrushchev. Khrushchev started to make concessions and if he hadn't been removed, that winter he was planning to go to Germany and to continue the genuine detente.

Let me remind you of the weakness of a man whose name is rarely associated with weakness—the weakness of Lenin. Lenin, when he came to power, in panic gave up to Germany everything Germany wanted. Just what it wanted. Germany took as much as it wanted and said, "Give Armenia to Turkey." And Lenin said, "Fine." It's almost an unknown fact but Lenin petitioned the Kaiser to act as intermediary to persuade the Ukraine and, thus, to make possible a boundary between the Communist part of Russia and the Ukraine. It wasn't a question of seizing the Ukraine but rather of making a boundary with the Ukraine.

We, we the dissidents of the USSR, don't have any tanks, we don't have any weapons, we have no organization. We don't have anything. Our hands are empty. We have only a heart and what we have lived through in the half century of this system. And when we have found the firmness within ourselves to stand up for our rights, we have done so. It's only by firmness of spirit that we have withstood. And if I am standing here before you, it's not because of the kindness or the good will of communism, not thanks to detente, but thanks to my own firmness and your firm support. They knew that I would not yield one inch, not one hair. And when they couldn't do more they themselves fell back.

This is not easy. In our conditions this was taught to me by the difficulties of my own life. And if you yourselves—any one of you—were in the same difficult situation, you would have learned the same thing. Take Vladimir Bukovsky, whose name is now almost forgotten. Now, I don't want to mention a lot of names because however many I might mention there are more still. And when we resolve the question with two or three names it is as if we forget and betray the others. We should rather remember figures. There are tens of thousands of political prisoners in our country and—by the calculation of English specialists —7,000 persons are now under compulsory psychiatric treatment. Let's take Vladimir Bukovsky as an example. It was proposed to him, "All right, we'll free you. Go to the West and shut up." And this young man, a youth today on the verge of death said: "No, I won't go this way. I have written about the persons whom you have put in insane asylums. You release them and then I'll go West." This is what I mean by that firmness of spirit to stand up against granite and tanks.

Finally, to evaluate everything that I have said to you, I would say we need not have had our conversation on the level of business calculations. Why did such and such a country act in such and such a way? What were they counting on? We should rather rise above this to the moral level and, say: "In 1933 and in 1941 your leaders and the whole western world, in an unprincipled way, made a deal with totalitarianism." We will have to pay for this, some day this deal will come back to haunt us. For 30 years we have been paying for it and we're still paying for it. And we're going to pay for it in a worse way.

One cannot think only in the low level of political calculations. It's necessary to think also of what is noble, and what is honorable—not only what is profitable. Resourceful western legal scholars have now introduced the term "legal realism." By legal realism, they want to push aside any moral evaluation of affairs. They say, "Recognize realities; if such and such laws have been established in such and such countries by violence, these laws still must be recognized and respected."

At the present time it is widely accepted among lawyers that law is higher than morality—law is something which is worked out and developed, whereas morality is something inchoate and amorphous. That isn't the case. The opposite is rather true! Morality is higher than law! While law is our human attempt to embody in rules a part of that moral sphere which is above us. We try to understand this morality, bring it down to earth and present it in a form of laws. Sometimes we are more successful, sometimes less. Sometimes you actually have a caricature of morality, but morality is always higher than law. This view must never be abandoned. We must accept it with heart and soul.

It is almost a joke now in the western world, in the 20th century, to use words like "good" and "evil." They have become almost old-fashioned concepts, but they are very real and genuine concepts. These are concepts from a sphere which is higher than us. And instead of getting involved in base, petty, short-sighted political calculations and games we have to recognize that the concentration of World Evil and the tremendous force of hatred is there and it's flowing from there throughout the world. And we have to stand up against it and not hasten to give to it, give to it, give to it, everything that it wants to swallow.

Today there are two major processes occurring in the world. One is the one which I have just described to you which has been in progress more than 30 years. It is a process of shortsighted concessions; a process of giving up, and giving up and giving up and hoping that perhaps at some point the wolf will have eaten enough.

The second process is one which I consider the key to everything and which, I will say now, will bring all of us our future; under the cast-iron shell of communism — for 20 years in the Soviet Union and a shorter time in other Communist countries—there is occurring a liberation of the human spirit. New generations are growing up which are steadfast in their struggle with evil; which are not willing to accept unprincipled compromises; which prefer to lose everything—salary, conditions of existence and life itself— but are not willing to sacrifice conscience; not willing to make deals with evil.

This process has now gone so far that in the Soviet Union today, Marxism has fallen so low that it has become an ancedote, it's simply an object of contempt. No serious person in our country today, not even university and high school students, can talk about Marxism without smiling, without laughing. But this whole process of our liberation, which obviously will entail social transformations, is slower than the first one—the process of concessions. Over there, when we see these concessions, we are frightened. Why so quickly? Why so precipitously? Why yield several countries a year?

I started by saying that you are the allies of our liberation movement in the Communist countries. And I call upon you: let us think together and try to see how we can adjust the relationship between these two processes. Whenever you help the persons persecuted in the Soviet Union, you not only display magnanimity and nobility, you're defending not only them but yourselves as well. You're defending your own future.

So let us try and see how far we can go to stop this senseless and immoral process of endless concessions to the aggressor—these clever legal arguments for why we should give up one country after another. Why must we hand over to Communist totalitarianism more and more technology—complex, delicate, developed technology which it needs for armaments and for crushing its own citizens? If we can at least slow down that process of concessions, if not stop it all together —and make it possible for the process of liberation to continue in the Communist countries—ultimately these two processes will yield us our future.

On our crowded planet there are no longer any internal affairs. The Communist leaders say, "Don't interfere in our internal affairs. Let us strangle our citizens in peace and quiet." But I tell you: Interfere more and more. Interfere as much as you can. We beg you to come and interfere.

Understanding my own task in the same way I have perhaps interfered today in your internal affairs, or at least touched upon them, and I apologize for it. I have traveled a lot around the United States and this has been added to my earlier understanding of it; what I have heard from listening to the radio, from talking to experienced persons.

America—in me and among my friends and among people who think the way I do over there, among all ordinary Soviet citizens—evokes a sort of mixture of feelings of admiration and of compassion. Admiration at the fact of your own tremendous forces which you perhaps don't even recognize yourselves. You're a country of the future; a young country; a country of still untapped possibilities; a country of tremendous geographical distances; a country of tremendous breadth of spirit; a country of generosity; a country of magnanimity. But these qualities—strength, generosity and magnanimity—usually make a man and even a whole country trusting, and this already several times has done you a disservice.

I would like to call upon America to be more careful with its trust and prevent those wise persons who are attempting to establish even finer degrees of justice and even finer legal shades of equality—some because of their distorted outlook, others because of short-sightedness and still others out of self-interest— from falsely using the struggle for peace and for social justice to lead you down a false road. Because they are trying to weaken you; they are trying to disarm your strong and magnificent country in the face of this fearful threat—one which has never been seen before in the history of the world. Not only in the history of your country, but in the history of the world.

And I call upon you: ordinary working men of America—as represented here by your trade union movement—do not let yourselves become weak. Do not let yourselves be taken in the wrong direction. Let us try to slow down the process of concessions and help the process of liberation!

Communism: A Legacy of Terror

Is it then possible or impossible to transmit the experience of those who have suffered to those who have yet to suffer? Can one part of humanity learn from the bitter experience of another or can it not? Is it possible or impossible to warn someone of danger?

How many witnesses have been sent to the West in the last 60 years? How many waves of immigrants? How many millions of persons? They are all here. You meet them every day. You know who they are: if not by their spiritual disorientation, their grief, their melancholy, then you can distinguish them by their accents by their external appearance. Coming from different countries and without consulting with one another, they have brought to you exactly the same experience; they tell you exactly the same thing: they warn you of what is already happening, what has happened in the past. But the proud skyscrapers stand on, point to the sky and say: it will never happen here. This will never come to us. It's not possible here.

It can happen. It is possible. As a Russian proverb says: "When it happens to you, you'll know it's true."

But do we really have to wait for the moment when the knife is at our throats? Couldn't it be

Address delivered in New York City on July 9, 1975. Sponsored by the American Federation of Labor-Congress of Industrial Organizations (AFL-CIO).

51

possible, ahead of time, soberly to assess the worldwide menace that threatens to swallow the whole
world? I was swallowed myself. I have been in the
dragon's belly, in the red burning belly of the
dragon. He wasn't able to digest me. He threw me
up. I have come to you as a witness to what it's
like there, in the dragon's belly.

It's an astonishing phenomenon that communism
has been writing about itself in the most open way—
in black and white—for 125 years. And even more
openly, more candidly in the beginning. The Communist Manifesto, for instance, which everyone knows
by name, and which almost no one ever takes the
trouble to read, contains even more terrible things
than what has actually been done. It's perfectly
amazing. The whole world can read, everyone is
literate, but somehow no one wants to understand.
Humanity acts in such a way as if it didn't understand
what communism is, and doesn't want to understand,
is not capable of understanding.

I think it isn't only a question of the disguises
which communism has assumed in the last decades.
It's rather that the essence of communism is quite
beyond the limits of human understanding. It's hard
to believe that people could actually plan such things
and carry them out. And precisely because its essence
is beyond comprehension, communism is so difficult
to understand.

In my last address in Washington I spoke a great
deal about the Soviet state system, how it was
created and what it is today. But it's perhaps more
important to discuss with you the ideology that inspired the system, that created it, and that still
governs it. It's much more important to understand
the essence of this ideology, and above all its legacy

which hasn't changed at all in 125 years. It hasn't changed since the day it was born.

That Marxism is not a science is something which is entirely clear to intelligent people in the Soviet Union. It would be a joke to call it some sort of science. Leaving aside the exact sciences, such as physics, mathematics, and the natural sciences, even the social sciences can predict an event—when in what way and how the event might occur. Communism has never made any such forecasts. It has never said where, when, and precisely what is going to happen. Nothing but declamations. Declamations to the effect that the world proletariat will overthrow the world bourgeoisie and the most happy and radiant society will then arise. The fantasies of Marx, Engels and Lenin break off at this point, not one of them goes any further to describe what the society would be like. They simply said: the most radiant, most happy society. Everything for the sake of man.

I wouldn't want to enumerate for you all the unsuccessful predictions of Marxism, but I can give a couple. For example, it was claimed that the conditions of the working class in the West would deteriorate steadily, get more and more unbearable until the workers would be reduced to total poverty. (If only in our country we could feed and clothe our working class, provide it with everything and give it as much leisure as you do!)

Or the famous prediction Communist revolutions would all begin in such advanced industrial countries as England, France, America, Germany—that's where communism will begin. (But it worked out exactly the other way, as you know.) Or the prediction that the socialist state wouldn't even exist. As soon as

capitalism would be overthrown, the state would at
once wither away. (Look about you: where can
you see states as powerful as in the so-called socialist
or Communist countries?) Or the prediction that
wars are inherent only to capitalism. Wars are said
to arise only because of capitalism; as soon as communism is introduced, all wars will come to an end.
(We have seen enough of this also: in Budapest, in
Prague, on the Soviet-Chinese border, in the occupation of the Baltic countries, and when Poland was
stabbed in the back. We have seen enough of this
already, and we will surely see more yet.)

Communism is as crude an attempt to explain
society and the individual as if a surgeon were to
perform his delicate operations with a meat-ax. All
that is subtle in human psychology and in the structure of society (which is even more delicate); all of
this is reduced to crude economic processes. This
whole created being—man—is reduced to matter. It's
characteristic that communism is so devoid of arguments that it has none to advance against its opponents in our Communist countries. It lacks arguments
and hence there is the club, the prison, the concentration camp, and insane asylums with forced confine-
ment.

Marxism has always opposed freedom. I will quote
just a few words from the founding fathers of
communism, Marx and Engels (I quote from the
first Soviet edition of 1929): "Reforms are a sign
of weakness" (vol. 23, p. 339); "Democracy is
more to be feared than monarchy and aristocracy,"
(vol. 2, p. 369); "Political liberty is a false liberty,
worse than the most abject slavery" (vol. 2, p. 394).
In their correspondence Marx and Engels frequently
said that after achieving power, terror would be

indispensable, that "it will be necessary to repeat the year 1793. After achieving power, we'll be considered monsters, but we couldn't care less" (vol. 25, p. 187).

Communism has never concealed the fact that it rejects all absolute concepts of morality. It scoffs at any consideration of "good" and "evil" as indisputable categories. Communism considers morality to be relative, to be a class matter. Depending upon circumstances and the political situation, any act, including murder, even the killing of thousands, could be good or could be bad. It all depends upon class ideology. And who defines class ideology? The whole class cannot get together to pass judgment. A handful of people determine what is good and what is bad. But I must say that in this very respect communism has been most successful. It has infected the whole world with the belief in the relativity of good and evil. Many people besides the Communists are carried away by this idea today. Among enlightened people it is considered rather awkward to use seriously such words as "good" and "evil." Communism has managed to instill in all of us that these concepts are old-fashioned concepts and laughable. But if we are to be deprived of the concepts of good and evil, what will be left? Nothing but the manipulation of one another. We will decline to the status of animals.

Both the theory and practice of communism are completely inhuman for that reason. There is a word very commonly used these days: "anti-communism." It's a very stupid word, badly put together. It makes it appear as though communism were something original, something basic, something fundamental. Therefore, it is taken as the point of departure, and anti-communism is defined in relation to communism. Here is why I say that this word

was poorly selected, that it was put together by people who do not understand etymology: the primary,
the eternal concept is humanity. And communism is
anti-humanity. Whoever says "anti-communism" is
saying, in effect, anti-anti-humanity. A poor construction. So we should say: that which is against communism is for humanity. Not to accept, to reject this
inhuman Communist ideology is simply to be a human
being. It isn't being a member of a party. It's a protest
of our souls against those who tell us to forget the
concepts of good and evil.

But what is amazing is that apart from all their
books, communism has offered a multitude of examples for modern man to see. The tanks have
rumbled through Budapest. It is nothing. The tanks
roar into Czechoslovakia. It is nothing. No one else
would have been forgiven, but communism can be
excused. With some kind of strange deliberation, as
though God wanted to punish them by taking away
their reason, the Communists erected the Berlin wall.
It is indeed a monstrous symbol that demonstrates
the true meaning of communism. For 14 years people
have been machine gunned there, and not only those
who wanted to leave the happy Communist society.
Recently some foreign boy from the western side
fell into the Spree River. Some people wanted to
pull him out, but the East German border guards
opened fire. "No, no, don't save him." And so he
drowned; this innocent boy.

Has the Berlin wall convinced anyone? No again.
It's being ignored. It's there, but it doesn't affect us.
We'll never have a wall like that. And the tanks in
Budapest and Prague, they won't come here either.
On all the borders of the Communist countries, the
European ones in any case, you can find electronic

killing devices. These are automatic devices for killing anyone who goes across. But people here say: "That doesn't threaten us either, we are not afraid of that." In the Communist countries they have a developed system of forced treatment in insane asylums. That's nothing. We're living quietly. Three times a day— right at this very moment—the doctors are making their rounds and injecting substances into peoples' arms that destroy their brains. Pay no attention to it. We'll continue to live in peace and quiet here.

There's a certain woman here named Angela Davis. I don't know if you are familiar with her in this country, but in our country, literally for one whole year, we heard of nothing at all except about Angela Davis. There was only Angela Davis in the whole world and she was suffering. We had our ears stuffed with Angela Davis. Little children in school were told to sign petitions in defense of Angela Davis. Little boys and girls, 8 and 9 years old in schools, were asked to do this. Well, they set her free. Although she didn't have a rough time in this country, she came to recuperate in Soviet resorts. Some Soviet dissidents—but more important, a group of Czech dissidents—addressed an appeal to her: "Comrade Davis, you were in prison. You know how unpleasant it is to sit in prison, especially when you consider yourself innocent. You now have such authority. Could you help our Czech prisoners? Could you stand up for those persons in Czechoslovakia who are being persecuted by the state?" Angela Davis answered: "They deserve what they get. Let them remain in prison." That is the face of communism. That's the heart of communism for you.

I would particularly want to remind you today that communism develops in a straight line and as a single entity, without altering as people now like to say. Lenin did indeed develop Marxism, but primarily along the lines of ideological intolerance. If you read Lenin, you will be astonished at how much hatred there was in him at the least deviation, whenever some view differed from his by so much as a hair's breadth. Lenin also developed Marxism in the direction of inhumanity. Before the October Revolution in Russia, Lenin wrote a book called "The Lessons of the Paris Commune." There he analyzed why the Paris Commune was defeated in 1871. And his principal conclusion was that the Commune had not shot, had not killed enough of its enemies. It had destroyed too few people, when it was necessary to kill entire classes and groups. And when he came to power, Lenin did just this.

And then the word Stalinism was thought up. It's a term which became very popular. Even in the West they often say now: "If only the Soviet Union doesn't return to Stalinism." But there never was any such thing as Stalinism. This was contrived by Khrushchev and his group in order to shift onto Stalin all of the characteristics and all the principal defects of communism. It was a very effective move. But in reality Lenin had managed to give shape to all the main aspects before Stalin ever came on the scene. It was Lenin who deceived the peasants about their land. He is the one who deceived the workers about self-management. He is the one who turned the trade unions into organs of oppression. He is the one who created the Cheka, the secret police. He is the one who created the concentration camps. It is he who sent troops out to the border areas to crush any national movements for liberation and to set up an empire.

The only new thing that Stalin did was based on mistrust. Where it would have been enough—in order to instill general fear—to jail two people, he would arrest a hundred. And those who followed Stalin have merely returned to the previous tactic: if it is necessary to send two off to jail, then send two, not a hundred. In the eyes of the party, Stalin's entire guilt lay elsewhere: he did not trust his own Communist Party. Due to this alone the concept of Stalinism was devised. But Stalin had never deviated from the same basic line. They used to sculpt a bas relief of Marx, Engels, Lenin and Stalin all together; to this one could add Mao Tse-tung, Kim Il Sung, Ho Chi Minh; they are all in the same line of development.

The following theory is also accepted in the West. It is said that China is a sort of purified, puritanical type of communism, one which hasn't been transformed for the worse. But China is simply a delayed phase of that so-called "war communism" established by Lenin in Russia, but which was in force only until 1921. Lenin established it not because the military situation required it, but because this is how they envisioned the future of their society. But when economic pressure required them to retreat, they introduced the so-called New Economic Policy and they retreated. In China this initial phase has simply lasted longer. China is characterized by all the same traits: massive compulsory labor which is not paid in accordance with its value; work on holidays; forced living in communes and the incessant drumming in of slogans and dogmas that abolish the human essence and deny all individuality to man.

What's worst in the world Communist system is its unity, its cohesion. Enrico Belinguer quite recently said that the sun had set on the Comintern. Not at all. It hasn't set. Its energy has been transformed

into electricity which is now pulsing through underground cables. The sun of the Comintern today
spreads its energy everywhere in the form of high-
voltage electricity. Quite recently there was an incident when western Communists indignantly denied
that Portugal was operating on instructions from
Moscow. Of course, Moscow also denied this. And
then it was discovered that those very orders had
been openly published in the Soviet magazine "Problems of Peace and Socialism." These were the very
instructions that Ponomarev had given. All the
seeming differences among the Communist parties of
the world are imaginary. All are united on one point:
your social order must be destroyed. Why should
we be surprised if the world doesn't understand this?
Even the socialists, who are the closest to communism,
don't understand this themselves. They cannot grasp
the true nature of communism. Recently, the leader
of the Swedish socialists, Olaf Palme, said that the
only way that communism can survive is by taking
the path of democracy. That is the same thing as
saying that the only way in which a wolf can survive
would be to stop eating meat and become a lamb.
And yet Palme lives right next door. Sweden is quite
close to the Soviet Union. I think that he, and
Mitterand, and the Italian socialists will live to the
day when they will be in the position that (Portugal's
Mario) Soares is in today.

Soares' situation today, by the way, is not yet at its
worst. An even more terrible future awaits him and
his party. Only the Russian socialists—the Menshe-
viks and the Socialist Revolutionaries—could have
told them of the fate that awaits them. But they cannot tell of it; they are all dead; they've all been killed.
Read the Gulag Archipelago for that.

Of course in the present situation the Communists have to assume various disguises. Sometimes we hear words like the "popular front," at other times "dialogue with Christianity" is brought up. For Communists to have a dialogue with Christianity! In the Soviet Union this dialogue was a simple matter: they used machine guns and revolvers. And today, in Portugal, unarmed Catholics are stoned by the Communists. This happens today. This is dialogue. . . And when the French and the Italian Communists say that they are going to have a dialogue, let them only achieve power and we shall see what this dialogue will look like.

When I traveled to Italy this past April, I was amazed to see hammers and sickles painted on the doors of churches, insults to priests scrawled on the doors of their houses. In general, offensive Communist graffiti cover the walls of Italian cities. This is today, at a time before they have achieved power. This is today . . . When their leaders were in Moscow, Palmiro Togliatti agreed to all of Stalin's executions. Just let them reach power in Italy and we shall see what the dialogue will look like then.

All of the Communist parties, upon achieving power, have become completely merciless. But at the stage before they achieve power, it's necessary to adopt disguises.

We Russians who have had experience with this, find it tragic to see what is going on in Portugal. We were always told, "Well, this happened to you Russians. It's just that you couldn't maintain democracy in your country. You had it for eight months and then it was throttled. That's eastern Europe for you." But look at Portugal, at the very western-most edge of Europe, you can't go further West than Portugal.

And what do we see there? We see a sort of caricature, a slightly altered version of what happened in
Russia. For us it sounds like a repetition. We recognize what's going on and can make the proper sub-
stitutions, placing our socialist in Soares' position.

Or another familiar note: in Russia the Bolsheviks
also pursued power under the slogan "All Power to
the Constituent Assembly." But when the elections
took place, they got 25 percent of the vote. So they
dispersed the Constituent Assembly. The Communists
in Portugal got 12 percent of the vote. So they made
their parliament entirely powerless. What irony: the
socialists have won the elections. Soares is the leader
of the victorious party. And he has been deprived of
his own newspaper. Just imagine: the leader of a
victorious party has been stripped of his own newspaper! And the fact that there an assembly has been
elected and that it will sit in session has no significance whatever. Yet the western press writes seriously
that the first free elections took place in Portugal.
Lord save us from such free elections!
     Specific instances of duplicity, of trickery, can of
course change from one set of circumstances to another. But we recognize the Communist character in
the episode when the Portuguese military leaders,
who are allegedly not Communists, decided to settle
the dispute within the newspaper "Republica" in the
following manner. "Come at 12 o'clock tomorrow,"
they said, "we'll open the doors for you and you
settle it all as you see fit." But they opened the doors
at 10 o'clock and for some reason only the Communists knew of this, but not the socialists. The Communists entered, burned all the incriminating documents and then the socialists arrived. Ah, yes, it was

of course only an error. An accident, they didn't check the time . . .

These are the sort of tricks—and there are thousands—which make up the history of our revolution. There will be many more such incidents in Portugal. Or take the following example: the current military leadership of Portugal, in order not to lose the assistance of the West (they have already ruined Portugal, there is nothing to eat, so they need help), have declared, "Yes, we shall keep our multi-party system." And the unfortunate Soares, the leader of the victorious party, now has to demonstrate that he is pleased with this declaration in favor of a multi-party system. But on the same day the same source declared that the construction of a classless society will begin immediately. Anyone who is the least bit familiar with Marxism knows that "classless society" implies that there won't be any parties. That is to say, on the very same day they said: there will be a multi-party system and we shall strangle every party. But the former is heard while the latter is inaudible. And everybody repeats only that there will be a multi-party system. This is a typical Communist technique.

Portugal has, in effect, fallen out of NATO today. I hate to be a prophet of doom but these events are irreversible. Very shortly Portugal will already be considered a member of the Warsaw Pact. It is painful to look at this tragic and ironic repetition of Communist techniques at the far ends of Europe, 60 years apart. In the same few months we see the throttling of a democracy which had only just begun to get on its feet.

The question of war is also well elucidated in Communist and Marxist literature. Let me show you how communism regards the question of war. I quote

Lenin: "We cannot support the slogan 'Peace' since we regard it as a totally muddled one and a hindrance to the revolutionary struggle." (Letter to Alexandra Kollontai, July 1915) "To reject war in principle is un-Marxist. Who objectively stands to gain from the slogan 'Peace'? In any case not the revolutionary proletariat." (Letter to Alexander G. Shliapnikov, November 1914). "There's no point in proposing a benign program of pious wishes for peace without at the same time placing at the forefront the call for illegal organization and the summons to Civil War." This is communism's view of war. War is necessary. War is an instrument for achieving a goal.

But unfortunately for communism, this policy ran up against your atomic bomb in 1945. The American atomic bomb. Then the Communists changed their tactics. Then they suddenly became advocates of peace at any cost. They started to convoke peace congresses, to circulate petitions for peace, and the western world fell for this deceit. But the goal, the ideology, remained the same. To destroy your society. To destroy the way of life known in the West.

But with your nuclear superiority, it wasn't possible to do this then. Hence they replaced one concept with another. They said: what is not war is peace. That is to say, they opposed war to peace. But this was a mistake. Only a part of the antithesis opposed to the thesis. Although an open war could not be conducted, they could still carry out their oppressions behind the scene—terrorism. Partisan war, violence, prisons, concentration camps. I ask you: is this peace?

The diametric opposite of peace is violence. And those who want peace in the world should remove not only war from the world, but also violence. If there is no open war, but there is still violence, that is not peace.

As long as in the Soviet Union, in China, and in other Communist countries there's no limit to the use of violence—and now we find India joining in (it appears that Indira Ghandi has learned a lot from her trip to Moscow; she has mastered these methods very well, and is now adding another 400 million persons to this continent of tyranny)—as long as there is no limit to this use of violence, as long as nothing restrains the use of violence over this tremendous land mass (more than half of humanity), how can you consider yourselves secure?

America and Europe together are not yet, I agree, an island in the ocean—I won't go so far as to say that. But America together with Europe is now a minority, and the process is still continuing. Until society in those Communist countries can keep a check on the government and can have an opinion on what the government does—now it doesn't even have the least idea of what the government is up to—until that time comes the West, and the world generally, has no guarantee at all.

We have another proverb in Russia: "Catch on you will when you're tumbling downhill."

I understand that you love freedom, but in our crowded world you have to pay a tax for freedom. You cannot love freedom just for yourself and quietly agree to a situation where the majority of humanity over the greater part of the globe is being subjected to violence and oppression.

The Communist ideology is to destroy your society. This has been their aim for 125 years and has never changed; only the methods have changed a little. When there is detente, peaceful co-existence, and trade, they will still insist: the ideological war must continue! And what is ideological war? It is a focus of hatred, this is continued repetition of the oath to destroy the western world. Just as, once upon a time in the Roman Senate, a famous speaker ended every speech with the statement: "Furthermore, Carthage must be destroyed," so today, with every act—detente, trade, or whatever—the Communist press, acting on secret instructions, sends out thousands of speakers who repeat: "Furthermore, capitalism must be destroyed."

I understand, it's only human that persons living in prosperity have difficulty understanding the necessity of taking steps—here and now, in a state of prosperity—to defend themselves. That even in prosperity one must be on guard.

But if I were to enumerate all the treaties that have been violated by the Soviet Union, it would take me another whole speech. I understand that when your statesmen sign some treaty with the Soviet Union or China you want to believe that it will be carried out. But the Poles who signed a treaty in Riga in 1921 with the Communists also wanted to believe that the treaty would be carried out, and they were stabbed in the back. Estonia, Latvia and Lithuania, who signed treaties of friendship with the Soviet Union, also wanted to believe that they would be carried out, but these countries were all swallowed.

And the persons who sign these treaties with you now—these very men and no others—at the same time give orders for persons to be confined in mental hospitals and prisons. Why should they be different? Do they have any love for you? Why should they act honorably and nobly toward you while they crush their own people? The advocates of detente have never yet explained this.

You want to believe and you cut down on your armies. You cut down on your research. There used to be an Institute for the Study of the Soviet Union—

at least there was one. (You know nothing about the Soviet Union. It's dark over there. These searchlights don't penetrate that far.) Knowing nothing, you eliminated the last genuine institute which actually could study this Soviet society, because there wasn't enough money to support it. But the Soviet Union is studying you. You are all wide open here, through the press and Congress. And they study you even more, increasing the size of their staffs. They follow what's going on in your institutions. They visit the buildings when they can; they even visit congressional committees; they study everything.

Of course, peace treaties are very attractive to those who sign them. They strengthen one's prestige with the electorate. But the time will come when the names of these public figures will be erased from history. Nobody will remember them any longer, but the western peoples will have to pay heavily for these over-trusting agreements.

Is it only a question of showing that detente is needed today, here and now? No. We have theoreticians who look very far into the future. The director of the Russian Institute of Columbia University, Marshall Shulman, at a meeting of the Senate Foreign Relations Committee, depicted a radiant long-range future, stating that detente would ultimately lead to cooperation between the United States and the USSR in the establishment of a world order. But what sort of new order, in cooperation with insatiable totalitarianism, does this professor want to see established? It won't be your order in any case.

But the principal argument of the advocates of detente is well-known: all of this must be done to avoid a nuclear war. But after all that has happened in recent years, I think I can set their minds at ease, and your minds at ease as well: there will not be any nuclear war. What for? Why should there be a nuclear war if for the last 30 years they have been breaking off as much of the West as they wanted— piece after piece, country after country and the process keeps going on. In 1975 alone four countries were broken off. Four—three in Indochina plus India, the process keeps going on, and very rapidly, too. One should be aware of how rapid the tempo is. But let us assume that ultimately the western world will understand and say, "No, not one step further." What will happen then?

Let me direct your attention to the following fact. You have theoreticians who say: "The U.S. must stop the process of nuclear armament. We have enough already. Today America has enough nuclear weapons to destroy the other half of the world. Why should we need more than that?" Let the American nuclear specialists reason this way if they want, but for some reason the nuclear specialists of the Soviet Union—and for some reason the leaders of the Soviet Union—think differently. Ask your specialists! Leave aside their superiority in tanks and airplanes— where they surpass you by a factor of four, five or seven. Take the SALT talks alone: in these negotiations your opponent is continually deceiving you. Either he is testing radar in a way which is forbidden by the agreement; or he is violating the limitations on the dimensions of missiles; or he is violating the limitations on their destructive force; or else he is violating the conditions on multiple warheads.

As the proverb says, "Look before you leap, or you will have bruises to keep."

At one time there was no comparison between the strength of the USSR and yours. Then it became equal to yours. Now, as all recognize, it is becoming superior to yours. Perhaps today the ratio is just greater than equal, but soon it will be 2 to 1. Then 3 to 1. Finally it will be 5 to 1. I'm not a specialist in this area, and you're not specialists either, I suppose, but this can hardly be accidental. I think that if the armaments they had before were enough, they would not have driven things further. There must be some reason for it. With such a nuclear superiority it will be possible to block the use of your weapons, and on some unlucky morning they will declare: "Attention. We're marching our troops to Europe, and if you make a move, we will annihilate you." And this ratio of 3 to 1, or 5 to 1 will have its effect: you will not make a move. Indeed, theoreticians will be found to say, "If only we can have that blessed silence . . ."

To make a comparison with chess; this is like two players who are sitting at a chess board, one of whom has a tremendously high opinion of himself and a rather low opinion of his opponent. He thinks that he will, of course, outplay his opponent. He thinks he is so clever, so calculating, so inventive, that he will certainly win. He sits there, he calculates his moves. With these two knights he will make four forks. He can hardly wait for his opponent to move. He's squirming on his chair out of happiness. He takes off his glasses, wipes them, and puts them back on again. He doesn't even admit the possibility that his opponent may be more clever. He doesn't even see that his pawns are being taken one after the other and that his castle is under threat. It all seems to him, "Aha, that's what we'll do. We'll set Moscow, Peking, Pyongyang, Hanoi one against the other."

But what a joke! No one will do any such thing! In the meantime, you've been outplayed in West Berlin, you've been very skillfully outplayed in Portugal. In the Near East you're being outplayed. One shouldn't have such a low opinion of one's opponent.

But even if this chess player were able to win the game on the board, carried away by the play, he forgets to raise his eyes; he forgets to look at his opponent and doesn't see that he has the eyes of a killer. And if the opponent cannot win the game on the board, he will take a club from behind his back and shatter the skull of the other chess player, winning the game in that way. This very calculating chess player also forgets to raise his eyes to the barometer. It has fallen. He doesn't see that it's already dark outside, that the clouds are coming on, that a hurricane is rising. That's what it means to be too self-confident in chess.

In addition to the grave political situation in the world today, we are witnessing the emergence of a wholly new situation, a crisis of unknown nature, one completely different, one entirely non-political. We're approaching a major turning point in world history, in the history of civilization. It can be seen in various areas by various specialists. I could compare it only with the turning point from the Middle Ages to the modern era, a whole shift of civilizations. It is a turning point at which settled concepts suddenly become hazy, lose their precise contours, at which our familiar and commonly used words lose their meaning, become empty shells, at which methods which have been reliable for many centuries no longer work. It's the sort of turning point at which the hierarchy of values to which we are dedicated all our lives, which we use to judge what is valuable and what is not, and which causes our lives and our hearts to beat, is starting to waver and may perhaps collapse.

And these two crises: the political crisis of today's world and the oncoming spiritual crisis, are occurring at the same time. It is our generation that will have to confront them. The leadership of your country, which is entering the third century of your national existence, will perhaps have to bear a burden greater than ever before seen in the whole of American history. Your leaders during this time (which is so near) will need profound intuition, spiritual foresight, high qualities of mind and soul. May God grant that in those times you will have at the helm in this country personalities as great as those who created your country.

In recent weeks, when traveling through various of your states, I of course felt that these two cities in which I have made my addresses—Washington and New York—are far from reflecting your country as a whole, with its tremendous diversity and all of its possibilities. Just as old St. Petersburg did not express the whole of Russia, just as Moscow does not reflect the Soviet Union of today, and just as Paris more than once abused its claim to represent all of France.

I was profoundly impressed by my contact with those places which are, and have always been, the wellsprings of your history. It really makes one think: the men who created your country never lost sight of their moral bearings. They did not laugh at the absolute nature of the concepts of "good" and "evil." Their practical policies were checked against that moral compass. And how surprising it is that a practical policy computed on the basis of moral considerations turned out to be the most far-sighted and the most salutary. Even though in the very short term one wonders: why all this morality? Let's just get on with the immediate job.

The leaders who created your country never said: "Let slavery reign right next door, and we will enter into detente with this slavery, so long as it doesn't come over to us."

I have traveled enough through the different states of your country and in its various regions to have become convinced that the American heartland is healthy, strong and broad in its outlook. I am convinced that these healthy, generous and inexhaustible forces will help you to elevate the whole style of your government leadership.

Yet, when one travels in your country and sees your free and independent life, all the dangers which I talked about today indeed seem imaginary. I've come and talked to people, and I see this is so. In your wide open spaces even I get a little infected. The dangers seem a little imaginary. On this continent it is hard to believe all the things which are happening in the world. But, gentlemen, this carefree life cannot continue in your country or in ours. The fates of our two countries are going to be extremely difficult, and it is better to prepare for this beforehand.

I understand, I sense that you're tired. You're fatigued, but you have not yet really suffered the terrible trials of the 20th century which have rained down on the old continent. You're tired, but not as tired as we are, lying crushed to the ground for 60 years. You're tired, but the Communists who want to destroy your system aren't tired; they're not tired at all.

I understand that this is the most unfavorable time to come to this country and to make this sort of address. But if it were a favorable time, if it were an appropriate time, there wouldn't be any need for me to speak.

Precisely because this is the worst possible time I have come to tell you about our experience over there. If our experience in the East could flow over to you by itself, it wouldn't be necessary for me to assume the unpleasant and inappropriate role of orator. I am a writer, and I would prefer to sit and write books.

But a concentration of world evil, of hatred for humanity is taking place and it is fully determined to destroy your society. Must you wait until it comes with a crowbar to break through your borders, until the young men of America have to fall defending the borders of their continent?

After my first address, as always, there were some superficial comments in the newspapers which did not really get to the essence. One of them was as follows: that I came here with an appeal to the United States to liberate us from communism. Anyone who has at all followed what I have said and written these many years, first in the Soviet Union and now in the West, will know that I've always said the exact opposite. I have appealed to my own countrymen— those whose courage has failed at difficult moments, and who have looked imploringly to the West—and urged them: "Don't wait for assistance, and don't ask for it; we must stand on our own feet. The West has enough troubles without us. If they support us, many thanks. But to ask for it, to appeal for it—never."

I said the last time that two processes are occurring in the world today. One is a process of spiritual liberation in the USSR and in the other Communist countries. The second is the assistance being extended by the West to the Communist rulers, a process of concessions, of detente, of yielding whole countries. And I only said: "Remember, we have to pull ourselves up—but if you defend us you also defend your own future."

We are slaves there from birth. We are born slaves. I'm not young anymore, and I myself was born a slave; this is even more true for those who are younger. We are slaves, but we are striving for freedom. You, however, were born free. If so, then why do you help our slave owners?

In my last address I only requested one thing and I make the same request now: when they bury us in the ground alive—I compared the forthcoming European agreement with a mass grave for all the countries of East Europe—as you know, this is a very unpleasant sensation: your mouth gets filled with earth while you're still alive—please do not send them shovels. Please do not send them the most modern earth-moving equipment.

By a peculiar coincidence the very day when I was giving my address in Washington, Mikhail Suslov was talking with your senators in the Kremlin. And he said, "In fact, the significance of our trade is more political than economic. We can get along without your trade." That's a lie. The whole existence of our slave owners from beginning to end relies on western economic assistance. As I said the last time, beginning with the first spare parts used to reconstruct our factories in the 1920s, from the construction in Magnitostroy, Dneprostroy, the automobile and tractor factories built during the first five-year plans, on into the postwar years and to this day, what they need from you is economically absolutely indispensable— not politically, but economically indispensable—to the Soviet system. The Soviet economy has an extremely low level of efficiency. What is done here by a few people, by a few machines, in our country takes tremendous crowds of workers and enormous masses of materials. Therefore the Soviet economy cannot deal with every problem at once: war, space (which is part of the war effort), heavy industry, light industry, and at the same time the necessity to feed and clothe its own population. The forces of the entire Soviet economy are concentrated on war, where you won't be helping them. But everything which is lacking, everything which is needed to fill the gaps, everything which is necessary to feed the people, or for other types of industry, they get from you. So indirectly you are helping them to rearm. You're helping the Soviet police state.

To get an idea how clumsy the Soviet economy is, I'll give you the following example: What kind of country is it, what kind of great power, which has tremendous military potential, which conquers outer space, but has nothing to sell? All heavy equipment, all complex and delicate technology, is purchased abroad. Then it must be an agricultural country? Not at all; it also has to buy grain. What then can we sell? What kind of economy is it? Can we sell anything which has been created by socialism? No! Only that which God put in the Russian ground at the very beginning, that's what we squander and that's what we sell. What we got from God in the first place. And when all this will come to an end, there won't be anything left to sell.

The president of the AFL-CIO, George Meany, has quite rightly said that it is not loans which the United States gives to the Soviet Union, it is economic assistance. It's foreign aid. It's given at a level of interest that is lower than what American workers can get for their home mortgages. That is direct aid.

But this is not all. I said in my last address and would like to repeat it again, that we have to look at every event from the other point of view—from the point of view of the Soviet Union. Our country is taking your assistance, but in the schools they're teaching and in the newspapers they are writing and in lectures they are saying, "Look at the western world, it's beginning to rot. Look at the economy of the western world, it's coming to an end. The great predictions of Marx, Engels and Lenin are coming true. Capitalism is breathing its last. It's already dead. And our socialist economy is flourishing. It has demonstrated once and for all the triumph of communism." I think, gentlemen, and I particularly address those of you who have a socialist outlook, that we should at last permit this socialist economy to prove its superiority. Let's allow it to show that it is advanced, that it is omnipotent, that it has defeated you, that it has overtaken you. Let us not interfere with it. Let us stop selling to it and giving it loans. If it's all that powerful, then let it stand on its own feet for 10 or 15 years. Then we will see what it looks like. I can tell you what it will look like. I am being quite serious now. When the Soviet economy will no longer be able to deal with everything, it will have to reduce its military preparations. It will have to abandon the useless space effort and it will have to feed and clothe its own people. And the system will be forced to relax.

Thus, all I ask you is that as long as this Soviet economy is so proud, so flourishing, and yours is so rotten and so moribund—stop helping it then. Where has a cripple ever helped along an athlete?

Another distortion appeared in your press with respect to my last address. Someone wrote that "one more advocate of the Cold War has come here. One more person has arrived to call on us to resume the Cold War." That is a misunderstanding. The Cold

War—the war of hatred—is still going on, but only on the Communist side. What is the Cold War? It's a war of abuse and they still abuse you. They trade with you, they sign agreements and treaties, but they still abuse you, they still curse you. In sources which you can read, and even more in those which are unavailable to you, and which you don't hear of, in the depths of the Soviet Union, the Cold War has never stopped. It hasn't stopped for one second. They never call you anything but "American imperialists." One day, if they want, all the Soviet newspapers could say that America wants to subjugate the world and our people would have nowhere to get any other information. Do I call upon you to return to the Cold War? By no means, Lord forbid! What for? The only thing I'm asking you to do is to give the Soviet economy a chance to develop. Do not bury us in the ground, just let the Soviet economy develop, and then let's see.

But can the free and varied western system follow this policy? Can all the western countries together say: "It's true, let us stop competing. Let us stop playing up to them. Let us stop elbowing each other and clamoring, 'Me, me, let me have a concession, please give it to me' . . ." It's very possible that this could not be done. And if this sort of unity cannot be achieved in the West, if, in the frenzied competition of one company with another they will continue to rush in loans and advanced technology, if they will present earth-moving equipment to our grave-diggers, then I'm afraid that Lenin will turn out to have been right. He had said: "The bourgeoisie will sell us rope, and then we shall let the bourgeoisie hang itself."

In ancient times trade would begin with the meeting of two persons who had come out of a forest or had arrived by sea. They would show one another that they didn't have a stone or club in their hand, that they were unarmed. And as a sign of this each extended an open hand. This was the beginning of the hand clasp. Today's word "detente" literally means a reduction in the tension of a taut rope. (What an ominous coincidence: A rope again!)

So "detente" means a relaxation of tension. But I would say that what we need is rather this image of the open hand. Relations between the Soviet Union and the United States of America should be such that there would be no deceit in the question of armaments, that there would be no concentration camps, no psychiatric wards for healthy people. Relations should be such that the throats of our women would no longer be constricted with tears, that there would be an end to the incessant ideological warfare waged against you, and that an address such as mine today would in no way be an exception.

People would simply be able to come to you from the Soviet Union, from China, and from other Communist countries and would be able to talk freely, without any tutoring from the KGB, without any special approval from the Central Committee of the Party. Rather, they would simply come of their own accord and would tell you the truth about what is going on in these countries.

This would be, I say, a period in which we would be able to present "open hands" to each other.

The Solzhenitsyn We Refuse to See

Arthur Schlesinger Jr.

> To you the Scholars of this College, who are here present before the Lord, I am concerned in my Spirit for you ... It is the Judgment of very Learned men, that in the Glorious Times promised to the Church on Earth, America will be Hell ... When you see this little Academy fall into the ground (as now it is shaking and most like to fall) then know it is a terrible thing which God is about to bring upon this Land.
>
> —Increase Mather at Harvard, 1697.

> Wherefore is all this evil come upon us? Is it not because we have forsaken the Lord? ... Do not our follies and iniquities testify against us? Have we not, especially in our Seaports, gone much too far into the pride and luxuries of life? Is it not a fact open to common observation, that profaneness, intemperance,, unchastity, the love of pleasure, fraud, avarice, and other vices, are increasing among us from year to year? ... Have our Statesmen always acted with integrity?
>
> —Samuel Langdon, president of Harvard, 1775.

The voice that echoed in Harvard Yard on June 8 would not have surprised the first several generations of Harvard men. For Alexander Solzhenitsyn renewed an ancient and, in those precincts, forgotten tradition of apocalyptic prophecy. Not only looking but sounding like a figure from the Old Testament, he preached an impassioned sermon, warning America of the progress of

Reprinted by permission from The Washington Post Outlook, *June 25, 1978.*

evil and the imminence of judgment, urging Americans to repent their sins, forsake their idols and prostrate themselves before the "Supreme Complete Deity."

Few men living have as clearly earned the right to assume the prophetic stance. Solzhenitsyn is a man of exemplary nobility and extreme bravery. A powerful novelist and an indispensable historian, he is an artist and moralist who has taken unto himself the suffering of his countrymen and has magnificently indicted a vile regime in the name of the Soviet peoples and of Russian history. When Solzhenitsyn speaks, the world has a duty to listen. But it must listen with care, understanding that prophecy has its own dogma and that prophets are not infallible. "The prophesying business," as Mencken said, "is like writing fugues; it is fatal to everyone save the man of absolute genius."

Solzhenitsyn's Harvard speech, like much prophetic utterance, lacks clear development of argument. Casual readers, instead of trying to disentangle the threads of his discourse, have seized upon his more sensational judgments, such as his assertion that "a decline in courage" is "the most striking feature which an outside observer notices in the West." This decline, he continued is "particularly noticeable among the ruling groups and the intellectual elite." It has led to a foreign policy founded on "weakness and cowardice." The American refusal to win the war in Vietnam, Solzhenitsyn declares, is a grievous and perhaps decisive example of the "loss of willpower in the West."

He finds the United States equally a failure at home. The "boundless space" granted "destructive and ir-responsible freedom" has resulted. Solzhenitsyn tells us, in an "abyss of human decadence," marked by the "revolting invasion of publicity, by TV stupor, and by intolerable music," by pornography, crime, and horror. The pervading legalism of American society has become a shoddy substitute for internal self-discipline.

Most dangerous of all, in his view, is the unconstrained freedom permitted the press. The mass media are corrupt and licentious, unwilling to confess or correct error, inundating the people with "superficial and misleading judgments" and an "excessive burdening flow of information." Yet "the press has become the greatest power within the western countries." "By what law has it been elected," Solzhenitsyn asks, "and to whom is it responsible?"

It is easy but pointless to note that Solzhenitsyn sounds rather like Gen. LeMay on Vietnam, like Pravda on American pornography and like Spiro T. Agnew on the American press. Certainly these and other items in his bill have struck responsive chords in many American breasts. But his specific charges cannot be easily divorced from his cosmic philosophy. One wonders how many who applaud his Harvard speech realize what a blanket endorsement of Solzhenitsyn implies.

Perhaps more people applaud Solzhenitsyn than read him. His Harvard jeremiad implied a broad set of judgments. The West went wrong, he believes, with the Renaissance and the 18th century Enlightenment. "We turned our backs upon the Spirit and embraced all that is material with excessive and unwarranted zeal."

Communism is an abomination, but so is capitalism. Commercial interest tended to "suffocate" spiritual life. Or, as he put it in 1973, "no incentive to self-limitation ever existed in bourgeois economics . . . It was a reply to the shamelessness of unlimited money-grubbing that socialism in all its forms developed." For all their differences, communism and capitalism are equally the end-products of "the logic of materialistic development."

Just as Solzhenitsyn's conservative admirers will reject his views on capitalism, so his liberal admirers will reject his views on democracy—views his great fellow-dissident, Andrei Sakharov, characterized in 1975 as "untrue and disturbing." Sakharov, for example, wants to liberalize and democratize the Soviet Union. He calls for a multi-party system and for the establishment of civil liberties. Little could be more remote from Solzhenitsyn's intentions. In 1975 he dismissed the Sakharov program as one more example of Russia's "traditional passive imitation of the West."

"A society in which political parties are active," he said, "never rises in the moral scale. . . . Are there no *extraparty* or *nonparty* paths of national development?" As for civil liberty, "the West," he wrote in 1969, "has supped more than its fill of every kind of freedom, including intellectual freedom. And has this saved it? We see it today crawling on hands and knees, its will paralyzed." (This was five years before he went into exile. His Harvard testimony therefore recorded not what he discovered after he came west but what he had always believed about the West.)

To regard freedom "as the object of our existence," he said in 1973, "is nonsense . . . There is, therefore, a miscalculation in the urgent pursuit of political freedom as the first and main thing." He finds it equally nonsensical to regard earthly happiness as the object of existence. At Harvard he expressly rejected the proposition that "man lives to be free and to pursue happiness. (See, for example, the American Declaration of Independence.)"

In short, Solzhenitsyn has no belief in what he called at Harvard "the way of western pluralistic democracy." People lived for centuries without democracy, he wrote in 1973, "and were not always worse off." Russia under authoritarian rule "did not experience episodes of self-destruction like those of the 20th century, and for 10 centuries millions of our peasant forbears died feeling that their lives had not been too unbearable." In "patriarchal" societies people "even experienced that 'happiness' we are forever hearing about." Moreover, they preserved the health of the nation—"a level of moral health incomparably higher than that expressed today in simian radio music, pop songs and insulting advertisements." Undermined by the cult of freedom, he said at Harvard, "administrative power has been drastically reduced in all western countries."

As against democracy, with its weakness, mediocrity and moral chaos, Solzhenitsyn prefers systems "based on subordination to authority."

His objection to the Soviet system, he has explained, is "not because it is undemocratic, authoritarian, based on physical constraint—a man can live in such conditions without harm to his spiritual essence." His objection is that "over and above its physical constraints, it demands of us total surrender of our souls." Authoritarian regimes *"as such* are not frightening—only those which are answerable to no one and nothing." The autocrats of religious ages "felt themselves responsible before God. . . . The autocrats of our own time are dangerous precisely because it is difficult to find higher values which would bind them."

Solzhenitsyn's ideal has nothing to do with liberal democracy. If asked whether he saw the West "as a model to my country, frankly I would have to answer negatively." His ideal is a Christian authoritarianism governed by God-fearing despots without benefit of politics, parties, undue intellectual freedom or undue concern for popular happiness. Repression, indeed, is good for the soul. "The need to struggle against our surroundings," he wrote in 1973, "rewards our efforts with greater inner success."

Even today the Soviet Union, he assures us, provides a healthier moral environment than the United States. "Through intense suffering our country has now achieved a spiritual development of such intensity," he said at Harvard, "that the western style in its present state of spiritual exhaustion does not look attractive." The superior moral weight and complexity of life in the

U.S.S.R. produce "stronger, deeper and more interesting characters than those generated by standardized Western well-being." Where the Declaration of Independence talked about life, liberty and the pursuit of happiness, Solzhenitsyn's essential thesis is strength through suffering.

For Solzhenitsyn, with his organic view of society, the nation even more than the individual is the crucial moral unit. Nations too can partake of the mystique of suffering. They "are very vital formations, susceptible to all moral feelings, including—however painful a step it may be—repentenance." In his fascinating essay, "Repentance and Self-Limitation in the Life of Nations," published in 1975, Solzhenitsyn argued that "repentance is now a matter of life and death," for the sake not merely of life beyond the grave but of "our very survival on this earth."

Repentance, he tells us, will lead nations on to the possibility of self-limitation. "Such a change will not be easy for the free economy of the West. It is a revolutionary demolition and total reconstruction of all our ideas and aims. . . . We must abjure the plague of expansion beyond out borders, the continuous scramble after new markets and sources of raw material, increases in our industrial territory or the volume of production, the whole insane pursuit of wealth, fame and change."

He condemns equally the foreign policy of his own country: "We are ready in our conceit to extend our responsibility to any other country, however distant . . . We meddle indefatigably in conflicts on every continent, lay down the law, shove people into quarrels, shamelessly push arms till they have become our most important item of export."

All this, he said, is catastrophically wrong. "Let us give up trying to restore order overseas, keep our grabbing imperial hands off neighbors who want to live their own lives. . . . We must stop running out into the street to join every brawl and instead retire virtuously into our own homes so long as we are in such a state of disorder and confusion." The nation must concentrate on its *inner* tasks: on healing its soul, educating its children, putting its own house in order. "Should we be struggling for warm seas far away, or ensuring that warmth rather than enmity flows between our citizens?"

These eloquent words might have come from speeches by George Kennan or George McGovern. Yet, when Americans repenting the excesses of Vietnam call for a policy of self-limitation, Solzhenitsyn, instead of rejoicing in converts, denounces them as cowards. Can he really believe that bombing Vietnamese back to the Stone Age is a test of courage?

Still, prophets are not always consistent. Perhaps, as a fervent Russian nationalist, he is more concerned with the salvation of Russia than of America. He should not be so contemptuous of Americans, who want to save their own souls. Or perhaps his is the understandable frustration of the messenger who tries to tell the West about the true nature of Soviet tyranny and encounters only blandness and complacency.

Before the Second World War Arthur Koestler wrote with comparable frustration about the inability of the victims of Nazism to make the British believe their personal testimony about Hitler's terror. Later Koestler decided that what the English lacked was not courage but imagination. No doubt it was this very lack of imagination that made Britain stand alone against Hitler after the fall of France. Maybe Solzhenitsyn understands the United States as little as Koestler understood the Britain of 1939.

In any event, Solzhenitsyn at Harvard was offering only fragments of a grand vision of the nature and destiny of man. Regeneration can come, for nations as well as for individuals, only through confession of sin and acknowledgement of the sovereignty of the Almighty. This vision would have been familiar to the Puritan divines who preached in Harvard Yard three centuries ago. It includes the premonitions of Armageddon, the final struggle with Satan. "The forces of Evil have begun their decisive offensive," Solzhenitsyn cried at Harvard. "You can feel their pressure." It partakes of the millenial dream as set forth in the books of Daniel and of Revelation. "If the world has not come to its end, it has approached a major turn in history . . . it will exact from us a spiritual upsurge."

This is a great, searching vision. In its majesty and profundity, in its perception of the evil inherent in human nature, it exposes the shallow religiosity of a born-again White House that, against every Augustinian and Calvinist insight, proclaims the doctrine of the inherent goodness of man and the aspiration to produce a government as good, decent virtuous, loving, etc., as the American people. The challenge to American smugness and hedonism, to the mediocrity of our mass culture, to the decline of self-discipline and civic spirit, is bracing and valuable.

To this extent Solzhenitsyn shares common ground with our Puritan ancestors. But Solzhenitsyn's faith is suffused, in addition, by the other-wordly mysticism of the Russian Church—a mysticism that reflected the political absolutism of Russian society. By Russian religious standards, earthly happiness is nothing compared to the divine judgment.

The Puritan tradition was more empirical. Even the New England ministry had to temper its conviction of divine sovereignty with concession to the rough democracy of a nonprescriptive society, where men made their way in life through their own labor. In the 18th century Calvinism absorbed John Locke and laid the philosophical basis for the American experiment in democracy.

This is why the two traditions diverged—why the Solzhenitsyn vision, with its fear of human freedom, its indifference to human happiness, its scorn for democracy, its faith in the authoritarian state, is so alien to the great tradition of the West. The greatest American theologian of our own time, Reinhold Niebuhr, demolished years ago the mystical illusion that nations have souls like individuals. Nor would he for a moment accept the authoritarian pretense that rulers, when avowing religious faith, are thereby rendered more immune than the rest of us to the corruptions of power. "The worst corruption," said Niebuhr, "is a corrupt religion"; and of course, "Man's capacity for justice makes democracy possible, but man's inclination toward injustice makes democracy necessary."

At Harvard Solzhenitsyn remarked that the West "never understood" Russia. One may respond that Solzhenitsyn has never understood America. He arrived complete with preconceptions about American decadence and cowardice and evidently nothing he has found in the mass media has disabused him. But, as Archibald MacLeish has well said, "What he knows of the Republic he knows not from human witnesses but from television programs, which present their depressing parody of American life to him as they present it also to us, but with this difference—that we know the parody for what it is."

He comes, moreover, as a messenger of God. "Truth eludes us," he said at Harvard, "if we do not concentrate with total attention on its pursuit." He has concentrated with total attention and does not doubt that the truth is his.

But the notion of absolute truth is hard for Americans to take. If absolute truth exists, it is certainly not something confided intact to frail and sinful mortals. Mr. Dooley long ago defined fanatics as men who do what they think "th' Lord wud do if He only knew the facts in th' case." And Jefferson in his first inaugural: "Sometimes it is said that man cannot be trusted with the government of himself. Can he, then be trusted with the government of others? Or have we found angels in the form of kings to govern him? Let history answer this question." History has answered this question with terrible certitude in the 20th century. "The unfortunate thing," Pascal said long before, "is that he who would act the angel acts the brute."

If prophecy is one Christian virtue, humility is another. Knowing the crimes committed in the name of a single Truth, Americans prefer to keep their ears open to a multitude of competing lower-case truths. Ours has been a nation of skepticism, experiments, accommodation, self-criticism, piecemeal but constant reform—a mixture of traits repugnant to the authoritarian and messianic personality, but perhaps not too bad for all that.

Americans were deemed as sinful in 1678 as Solzhenitsyn deems them in 1978; the Day of Judgment was quite as near and remote then as now. We welcome his presence and honor his witness; but he must understand the irrelevance of his grand vision to a democratic and libertarian society. Emerson, as usual, said it best:

> *I like the church, I like a cowl,*
> *I love a prophet of the soul;*
> *And on my heart monastic aisles*
> *Fall like sweet strains or pensive smiles;*
> *Yet not for all his faith can see*
> *Would I that cowled churchman be.*

A New Type of Soviet Resistance?

Alex Simirenko

In the tradition of my ancestors, a Zaporozhian cossack personified all the virtues that a man can possess. Ukrainian folklore is rich with tales about the cossack Mamai, a mythical figure who always appeared from nowhere to save the day. He is said to have been a fearless defender of faith and virtue and a protector of the frail and the sick. He could be either gentle or tough, but always he fought against evil, for he lived in a world in which distinctions between good and evil were not yet blurred. For a while and at a distance, Solzhenitsyn appeared to many of us as that legendary Mamai. It was shocking to discover that he was an ordinary mortal.

As the legend of the man began to recede, we were at least happy to discover that he had cossack qualities. As the proverb says, a cossack is one who swims against the current: Solzhenitsyn is the epitome of such a swimmer. One would still like to think that what appears to be character flaws, as revealed in his speech to the American Federation of Labor and Congress of Industrial Organizations (AFL-CIO), are due mainly to haste, harassment, inadequate time to ponder a statement, the need to drive home a point to a mass audience or possibly a poor translation. Henry Adams's observation that ''no one means all he says, and yet few say all they mean'' seems to be singularly apt in the present situation.

However, much of what Solzhenitsyn says about dissent in the Soviet Union is directly relevant to the nature of legitimation of the Soviet regime and its acceptance or rejection by the governed. When we look at the history of the Soviet Union from the standpoint of the legitimation of its regime, or, in other words, the legitimation of the Communist party as its ruling body, we find that most of the official dates are not very appropriate to the task. Legitimate authority cannot even be said to have been established on December 30, 1922, the date for the establishment of the Soviet Union. The regime encountered a prolonged armed resistance at least until about 1928 and that entire period, beginning with the October Revolution, may be more properly considered the period of formation. Since 1928, three distinct phases in the legitimation process can be discerned, with the first two running a cycle of twenty years:

1. The Period of Opposition   (1928-1948)
2. The Period of Dissent   (1948-1968)
3. The Period of Noncompliance (1968-   )

Considerable literature has now accumulated dealing with the Period of Opposition; the best known is Solzhenitsyn's *The Gulag Archipelago*. We also have learned much from reading the memoirs of Nadezhda Mandelstam, Zhores Medvedev's *The Rise and Fall of T.D. Lysenko*, Roy Medvedev's *Let History Judge*, David Joravsky's *The Lysenko Affair*, Robert Conquest's *The Great Terror* and Borys Levytsky's *The Uses of Terror*. In addition to these well-known works, we have vast documentation of the period by World War II emigrés whose stories have been largely ignored in the West, even at the height of the cold war.

The regime's opponents during this phase differed significantly from the resistance of the two later periods. Members of the early opposition believed that they were confronting the stupidity and intolerance of brazen and ruthless people, rather than "evil." They did not seek martyrdom and would have been happy to avoid it if they could. They were modest but proud people doing their job and endeavoring to retain their integrity. They would have considered it unmitigated gall to expect people from other countries to make sacrifices for the sake of liberating them. They fervently believed that fighters against other tyrannies, including non-Communist tyrannies, were engaged in an equally valid struggle. The idea that some torturers are better (less ''evil'') than others would have been quite repugnant to them.

Dissenter as Martyr

The Dissent Period parallels that of the cold war, in the course of which the words dissent, dissenter and dissident became popular. Solzhenitsyn himself is a product of the Dissent Period and his present writing is most representative of that period.

The dissenter in this mold can be seen almost as a caricature of the early opponents of the regime. He is a martyr who feels that only his cause and suffering are to be attended to, since he is sacrificing himself for the rest of humanity in the fight against evil at the very source of that evil. The dissenter is a creature of hope because he relies upon others for the ulitmate overthrow of the regime. As Solzhenitsyn has aptly put it: ''Interfere as much as you can. We beg you to come and interfere.'' The cold war seems to have actually stifled an opposition based on self-reliance. It also furnished the regime with the best weapon to fight dissenters. It became all too easy to accuse them of aiding and abetting foreigners against the motherland. Worst of all, the cold war created the false hope among the dissenters that liberation could somehow be achieved with someone else's help, as if that someone would not dictate the terms of liberation.

The cold war period is yet to be studied in depth by historians and our statements about its effect upon the resistance movement must be regarded as conjectural and tentative. We may come to see the cold war as the period which ensured the survival of the Party and, consequently, the survival of the Soviet system. It is doubtful that the same case can be made as far as the survival of the capitalist system is concerned. The kind of expansion and development of capitalism made possible by the cold war has brought in its wake military defeat, fiscal crisis and civil turmoil. Solzhenitsyn is certainly right in asserting that the scorecard tally stands in favor of the Soviet regime.

Destruction of Hope

The invasion of Czechoslovakia, in August, 1968, may be perceived as the major event transforming the nature of Soviet resistance to the Party. The date symbolizes the destruction of hope among Soviet resisters, which has forced them into an uncompromising position. As Solzhenitsyn says, the new détente-period dissenter is "not willing to accept unprincipled compromises." These resisters, unlike those of the two earlier periods, reject the Party's claim for legitimacy. Petitions to Stalin or the various bureaus of the government and letters to Brezhnev, such as the one written by Solzhenitsyn, are quite out of character for noncompliant individuals. The same is true of picketing and demonstrations. Noncompliant individuals assume that the Party has no right to govern and consequently go about their lives as though the Party did not exist, irrespective of the danger this may present to their personal safety.

Although this new unobtrusive behavior will not provide stories and pictures for foreign correspondents, it will give the movement the legitimacy of a genuine opposition which cannot be accused of being in the pay of foreigners. Since much of the dynamism of the new movement is based on bitter feelings of Western betrayal, as reflected in some of Solzhenitsyn's statements, it should be able to gain "converts" among those sections of the population that could not possibly have been attracted to the idea before, especially sons and daughters of persons in influential positions.

Resistance through noncompliance is actually not a new phenomenon in the Soviet Union. It has been practiced widely since the Revolution among the various minority groups, particularly the non-Russian nationalists and members of various religious groups. Now it has penetrated into Russian chauvinist circles, where there is access to persons with power and influence. It would not be surprising if the Party, confronted by this new threat and in a desperate effort at survival, were to reverse its Russian nationalist position in favor of a more genuine internationalism. Quite the opposite scenario may be envisioned as well. Clues to the future will come at the next Party Congress with the unfolding of plans for the revised Constitution.

Warning Cry

There is little doubt that Solzhenitsyn has correctly perceived the determination of the new resistance in not complying with the will of the Party and the inherent dangers which lie ahead. In the past, it has always been difficult to establish the basic incompetence of the Party, contrary to its claim to scientific knowledge in running the country, because it has always found a variety of scapegoats while maintaining its own inviolability. In early periods, there were foreign intrigues on the outside and remnants of past mentality on the inside. In more recent years, the blame was placed on cold war machinations on the outside and the incompetence of various professionals on the inside. Presently, with "détente" in full bloom, foreigners cannot be that easily blamed and the professionals are themselves demanding that the Party demonstrate its own competence.

Solzhenitsyn's words of distress reflect his concern with United States policy toward the Soviet Union in the event that détente might lead to "destabilization" of the Party, a situation for which we are completely unprepared, at least on the level of public opinion. Solzhenitsyn may rightly wonder if we would find it in our national interest to aid the Party in its crisis. The West is already selling technological know-how to the Soviet Union which will make it easier for the Party to control its dissidents; this presumably includes interrogation equipment of various kinds as well as mail inspection techniques. Should the National Security Council decide, in the heat of rapidly unfolding events, that we would rather deal with the stable and predictable (albeit incompetent) Party instead of a military junta or a new regime composed of dissidents hostile to the West, would it not be conceivable that we would be willing to share our knowledge of counterinsurgency techniques as well?

At this point, it is only fair to reassure Solzhenitsyn that nothing of the sort will happen—not because it could not happen—but because we will not permit it to happen. Only genuine and lasting noninterference in the internal affairs of the Soviet Union or, in Solzhenitsyn's words, a complete and total betrayal of Eastern Europe, is likely to bring about the collapse of the Party through the noncompliance of people under its control. A variety of external and internal pressures, both political and economic, would prevent our participation in such a "betrayal." It is not in our nature to regard ourselves as so completely devoid of compassion as a genuine friendship with the Party would demand. Nor is it in our interest to bring up our children in that cynical spirit. We have come close to losing our children once before.

Future of Détente

Under these circumstances, our halfhearted and vacillating commitment to détente will continue until 1988, (projecting a twenty-year cycle), by which time a new configuration of power in Europe and the world should have made itself felt. Meanwhile, in the Soviet Union, noncompliant individuals "not willing to sacrifice conscience," will continue to make their quiet, defiant stand. For others the road of redemption through martyrdom will remain. A few Soviet subjects will be permitted to escape the system, raising hopes in the hearts of others that they too may have a chance if only they push the right combination of buttons. As in Pavlov's experiment, when the subjects refused to believe that the buttons were not wired up, so will most Soviet subjects refuse to believe that the Party does not have their lives wired up and under control at all times.

American citizens reading local papers and watching television newscasts may be growing increasingly confused about détente, Helsinki and our relationship with the Communist systems. They are already sufficiently puzzled by the fact that the West is presently host not only to Solzhenitsyn, but also to Svetlana, the daughter of his former jailer Stalin, both of whom, to top it off, are rumored to be millionaires. Perhaps, in the end, this is the hidden message of that rather enigmatic (Russian?) proverb which says that the cloth unravels from the edge.

Return to
the Cold War

Melvin Gurtov

L ike a twentieth-century Citizen Genet, Aleksandr Solzhenitsyn brings to America an appeal for overhauling the
Nixon-Ford-Kissinger strategy of détente with the Soviet
Union. In simplest terms, Solzhenitsyn would like us to get
tough with the Russians (again) and bear the mantle of "Free
World" leader with renewed pride. He does not appreciate
the narrow "realism" which the present administration, like
previous ones, insists is the only reasonable basis on which to
conduct foreign policy.

Although Solzhenitsyn is not welcome at the White House
these days, administration leaders are probably not entirely
unhappy with his speech. Insofar as he wants to see the
United States preeminent again in world affairs, he is very
much attuned to the spirit of recent high-level policy statements. Solzhenitsyn's brief survey of the cold war—which is
far more deserving of the description "revisionist" than most
writing so called—is also probably acceptable to the President and his Secretary of State. What is most disturbing about
Solzhenitsyn's remarks is that, right on the heels of Vietnam,
they are being so politely received, even applauded in some
quarters. While in Congress neoisolationists win occasional
victories, across the country there seems to be a conservative,
internationalist backlash in which our distinguished Russian

visitor now has a part. This is why his speech is important to debate.

Morality and Humanism

Reminiscent of John Foster Dulles, Solzhenitsyn speaks of morality, humanism and high principle in the conduct of foreign affairs, yet he accepts increased conflict in their name. In suggesting that the United States become ''allies of our liberation movement in the Communist countries,'' ''interfere more and more'' in Soviet internal affairs and be more demanding in negotiations with the Russians, Solzhenitsyn is fueling another anti-Communist crusade. He seems content to have the United States return to strategies of confrontation that eventuated in Vietnam: containment, rollback, brinkmanship and ''liberal'' interventionism. The implication, if not the direct consequence, of his proposals is the return of the cold war to its most frigid phase.

Solzhenitsyn's contentions emerge from a fundamental misappraisal of cold war history and of its two major protagonists. His is a black-and-white portrayal that makes American foreign policy seem so magnanimous and innocent as to embarrass even a State Department speech writer. Overwhelmed by his experiences with Stalinist terror and the continuing attacks on intellectual freedom under Brezhnev and Kosygin, he has cast the Union of Soviet Socialist Republics as the consistent villain in international politics. The Union of Soviet Socialist Republics gobbles up countries at will, uncontested; it is imperialism on the rampage, a worldwide monolith led by an all-powerful, single-minded party. As for the United States, he seems unaware of the American share of responsibility for bringing on the cold war between 1945 and 1947; of the numerous United States interventions in the Third World; of the long period of hostility toward China; of the ''lost crusade'' in Indochina (is the *Pentagon Papers* unavailable in Russian?); and, within the

United States, of Watergate and various economic "crises" manipulated by corporate blocs. His blinders allow him to see only a backtracking, appeasing America—a pitiful, helpless giant.

Lesson of Vietnam

For Solzhenitsyn, the lesson of Vietnam appears to be not the wisdom of restraining the exercise of power, but the necessity of using it again and again. He would like the United States to recover the firmness that marked its policies in Korea and during the Cuban missile crisis. (One recalls Walt Rostow similarly urging Lyndon Johnson to remember Berlin and Cuba as the bombing campaign moved into high gear in 1965.) Perhaps Solzhenitsyn is not familiar with the kind of regime in Seoul that the United States now supports (with nuclear threats, no leşs) as a result of the Korean War. Nor has he considered that the missile "crisis" need never have occurred. The Soviet leaders put missiles into Cuba to offset the substantial intercontinental ballistic missile (ICBM) gap that had developed in America's favor. Kennedy overreacted to a "threat" he later admitted was political and psychological, not military.

Despite disagreements with Solzhenitsyn's interpretations, common ground can still be found with his critique of the United States strategy for détente. For that strategy is indeed "a caricature of morality." Kissinger's notion of realism amounts to moderating portions of the cold war competition (e.g., by limiting nuclear testing, antiballistic missiles [ABMs] and strategic systems, recognizing the postwar division of Europe, increasing trade and credits, holding joint scientific ventures) while continuing it, with no basic change in ideology or interest, in other areas (e.g., the Middle East, nuclear and missile development, military power in the Indian Ocean). Looking at American behavior in recent years in Bangladesh, Chile and Portugal, one is hard put to distinguish the "new" balance-of-power politics from the "old" power politics.

Jet-speed diplomacy and a series of agreements between the two superpowers have helped create the impression that the cold war is over. Solzhenitsyn is correct to say it is not, but it is a gross distortion for him to assign the Soviet leadership sole responsibility. Surely the "true détente" he wants—one based on domestic and international disarmament, control over government actions by a vigilant press and parliament and termination of ideological warfare—requires major changes in the process and content of foreign policy for the United States, no less than for the Soviet Union. For it is pretense to imply that American arms are not being used for domestic and international repression (the arms industry recorded foreign sales of $8 billion last year); that the United States has not been rapidly developing new weapons and delivery systems since the Moscow and Vladivostok agreements were signed; that Congress, the press and the public are single-mindedly and successfully containing executive power (witness, for instance, the flouting of the War Powers Resolution in the *Mayaguez* incident); and that the United States does not engage in ideological warfare.

Solzhenitsyn says the liberation of the human spirit is the quest of the Russian people (for whom he presumes to speak). Does he not also think that is the quest of most Americans? Having just arrived here, perhaps he is unaware of how widespread feelings of alienation, dehumanization, frustration and deprivation are in our Great Society. Liberation is the critical problem of our time; it is a common need of all peoples because of the increasing oppressiveness of the corporate state, whatever the form of its government might be called. That liberation cannot come from without. External intervention—for that is what United States liberalizing pressure would amount to—exacerbates tensions, invites harsher repression, leads to counterintervention and inevitably comes to be resented precisely by those who are "rescued" when they realize the intervention has not really liberated anyone, least of all their spirits. The proper business of the government of the United States, Mr. Solzhenitsyn, is to help its own people liberate themselves.

In Defense of Détente

Lynn Turgeon

The heart of Aleksandr Solzhenitsyn's bizarre rewriting of history goes back to the significance of the rise of national socialism in Germany in 1933 and the eventual historical alliance between the Western countries and the Soviet Union which was required to defeat the Axis powers. Thus he advocates our admission that "in 1933 and in 1941 your leaders and the whole Western World, in an unprincipled way, made a deal with totalitarianism."

Does this somewhat cryptic reference to 1933 refer to our acceptance of the rise of Hitlerian authoritarianism— achieved, it should be remembered, within a bourgeois democratic framework—or simply to the belated formal diplomatic recognition of the Soviet Union by Roosevelt? Presumably the latter, but in either case, it would seem that if any deal were made by the West with authoritarianism, it was made at Munich in 1938. As for the wartime alliance in 1941, this was forged primarily by the Nazis and Japanese through their respective attacks on the Ukraine and Pearl Harbor in June and December of that year. It is possible to argue—as have A.J.P. Taylor and Bruce Russett—that World War II was avoidable, at least for the United States, but this interpretation requires an evaluation that the British and French overreacted to Hitler's invasion of Poland and the liberation of former German territories.

At any rate, it is hardly true that England, France and the United States were the victors in World War II. The role of France was ambiguous at best, while the role of the Soviet Union in defeating Hitler was of paramount importance. While the Soviet Union was certainly deserving of aid after World War II, in recognition of the fact that the Soviet Union suffered by far the greatest losses, a request for a paltry $1 billion loan was mysteriously "lost" on a desk of the United States Department of State in 1945, and the reparations vaguely promised at Yalta and Potsdam were forgotten after the "successful" use of the A-bomb at Hiroshima. They were only eventually forthcoming as a result of Soviet "self-reliance" in the Soviet zone of Germany, Hungary, Romania and Bulgaria—all of whom had contributed their share to the destruction of Soviet property and lives.

High Living Standards

As for the fate of the Estonian, Latvian and Lithuanian peoples, it is difficult for this recent observer of the Baltic area to muster up any great sympathy for their "plight." As a generalization, these republics today enjoy the highest living standards in the Soviet Union; constitute a region where the individual non-Russian cultures are flourishing in the arts; and enjoy religious freedom which can be witnessed every Sunday in the great cathedrals of Kaunas, Vilnius and Riga. The independent Baltic states in the interwar years were hardly models of bourgeois democracy and, being capitalist in their orientation, were adversely affected by the Great Depression. It is no exaggeration to say that these talented peoples have never enjoyed comparable well-being—thanks primarily to their peaceful full employment operations under the Soviet nuclear umbrella.

While it is possible to document the spread of the non-capitalist system since World War II, this is hardly synonymous with the spread of Soviet influence. This is most dramatically evident in the Peoples Republic of China, but socialist nationalism—rather than Soviet internationalism—seems to be dominant in most of the countries which have abandoned capitalism as an economic system. Like most East Europeans, Solzhenitsyn is not too well informed about other socialist countries and therefore assumes that the impact of the Communist party of the Soviet Union outside the Russian Soviet Federated Socialist Republic is the same as it has been in Russia proper.

As in the Baltic republics, the local cultural life and institutional deviation from the Soviet Union is impressive in Eastern Europe: new churches are being built in Poland; private religious instruction—both Jewish and Catholic—prevails in Hungary; competing candidates appear on Hungarian ballots; Hungarian "new leftists" write for Western publications; Czech and Hungarian mothers are paid rather handsomely to stay at home with their children under three; homosexuality is legalized in the German Democratic Republic (GDR), Poland and Czechoslovakia; private enterprise continues in Hungary and in the GDR; Romanians refrain from taking part in Warsaw Pact maneuvers and even ask for United States arms; East European rock groups compete in the West, win honors, return home and so forth.

Soviet Concentration Camps

Solzhenitsyn seems to assume that Americans are unaware of the horrors and extent of Soviet concentration camps, whereas we had been through Gulag Archipelago at least twenty-five years ago when David Dallin and others documented the fact that twenty million Soviet citizens were imprisoned in Stalin's concentration camps after World War II. This was the same era when Secretary of State John Foster Dulles tried to convince us—using the same high moralistic tone as Solzhenitzyn—that it was our crusade to stop and roll back the "red tide." Dulles's refusal to sign the Geneva Accords in 1955 laid the groundwork for the most unfortunate involvement of the United States armed forces in our entire history. Fortunately, the possible nuclear holocaust has thus far been avoided due to sober calculations on the part of both United States and Soviet policymakers, the most important of whom have been John F. Kennedy and Richard M. Nixon on one hand, and Nikita Khrushchev and Leonid Brezhnev on the other.

As for the magnanimous behavior of the United States in the event of natural disasters, many of our citizens are no doubt quite selfless. But it should be pointed out that our foreign aid programs regularly fail to receive a majority support in Gallup polls. Our institutional generosity—as reflected in the constantly rising year-to-year shipments under foreign aid programs—reflects a systemic difference, one which is foreign to the noncapitalist system. All of these unrequited movements of goods and services create jobs and profits within our underutilized economy so that they are relatively costless given the real alternatives. This same phenomenon can also be seen domestically within the United States economy where areas subjected to floods and earthquakes are ultimately oases of relative prosperity due to the destruction of capital and the federal subsidies to certified disaster areas.

United States capitalists also understand the functionalism of such unexplicable events as lower interest rates on loans to the socialist bloc. The substantial export surpluses of the United States with socialist countries, including China, are a source of added employment and profits for United States workers and capitalists. Labor leaders—as evidenced by their refusal to load grain for the Soviet Union or even by their invitation to Solzhenitsyn—are a bit slower than our capitalists to recognize which side their bread is buttered on. But historic forces for change should eventually bring them around to supporting and enjoying a policy of détente.

As bad as things are in the Soviet Union in the eyes of Western intellectuals, it must be recognized that repression today is far less than it was under Stalin. In those days, a hard-line policy similar to that advocated by Solzhenitsyn was being pursued by the United States, particularly during the Truman era. It is probably no coincidence that the domestic atmosphere for our own intellectuals is also better today than during the McCarthy years when the hard-line against the Soviet Union was the rule.

Intervening in
the Soviet Union

Amitai Etzioni

It is sad to conclude that a man such as Alexander Solzhenitsyn, who is so evocative emotionally and historically, as
well as personally courageous, is nonetheless so wrong-
headed in his counsel to the United States as to how it should
deal with the Soviet Union and other Communist countries.
That hideous crimes against the people were committed in the
Soviet Union by the nation's leaders from 1918 through the
Stalinist era is indisputable. It is also true that in its desire to
have the Soviet Union as its ally in defeating Hitler, the
United States was very likely guilty of downplaying these
crimes.

Clearly, not all such tyrannical behavior has vanished from
the Soviet earth. Soviet harassment of Jews is a case in point.
It is important to ask, however, whether Soviet tyranny has
not undergone significant moderation in the quarter century
since Stalin's death? Was there not much greater use of
brutality by earlier generations of Soviet leaders than those
presently in power? Solzhenitsyn never addresses this question squarely. I file with those who hold that such a relaxation
of tyranny has occurred.

The next question is what is the best way to encourage
additional liberalization in the Soviet policy? Would it be by

excommunicating the Soviet Union through withdrawal of diplomatic recognition, curtailing trade and other exclusive measures or by seeking to involve the Soviet Union ever more deeply in the world community? To excommunicate a nation is to take a clear moral stand, but experience suggests that, in the past, such action has had little, if any, effectiveness in promoting freedom and may well be counterproductive. No Communist regime has ever collapsed because the United States refused to recognize or trade with it, while the fear engendered in the nation's leaders concerning possible United States military intervention may actually have caused a tightening of internal repression.

Governmental Criminality

In the world we live in we must, unfortunately, tolerate governmental criminality in other nations—up to a point. Genocide must surely not be permitted. But a great deal that we find morally reprehensible must be counteracted by dealing with, rather than merely condemning, the culprit. Drawing the line between when we should intervene, excommunicate or dialogue often proves agonizing. Yet, without some such line, the alternative is to wage a holy war against most of the world—not only Communist countries, but also South Africa, Rhodesia, Paraguay, Brazil, South Korea and Uganda.

If nations were to be barred from sitting down at the international bargaining table or participating in the world community on the basis of their past sins against democracy and human rights, then the United States would also be prohibited from taking a seat. In light of the fact that the Soviet Union is presently not a genocidal sinner, we could best work to further humanize it (and others, including our own nation) by greater—not lesser—involvement with each other.

The Prophet's Wrong Message

Richard Lowenthal

Aleksandr Solzhenitsyn is a great writer and one of the outstanding moral personalities of our time. He has told us many important truths and has done much to sharpen our awareness of human suffering in the countries under Communist rule and of our duty towards its victims. But I have read his Washington speech with feelings mixed of fascination, amazement and shock: fascination at the nearly seemless consistency of his vision of world affairs, amazement at its utter disaccord with the facts of recent international history and shock at the radical moral wrongness of the position he has now taken on questions upon which the survival of mankind may depend.

My shock at finding myself in almost total disagreement with Solzhenitsyn's views on the past, present and future of Western relations with the Soviet Union is all the greater because I agree with him on one fundamental issue—the totally evil nature of totalitarianism in all forms. I have come to know that nature both because I was a Communist in my student days in the 1920s and felt the horrors of the Stalinist purges of the 1930s as a personal crisis even long after I had broken with the Communist party, and because I lived through the rise of Nazi power in Germany and tried to fight it in an underground resistance group and later in exile. I have not personally suffered from totalitarian persecution, but many of the friends of my youth have perished in the prisons and camps of Hitler and Stalin; these experiences have had a formative impact on my political outlook and on my interests as a scholar. Thus I believe I understand the cause that Solzhenitsyn has at heart.

The difference between us is not that Solzhenitsyn looks at Western policies as a moralist and I as a student of international affairs, but resides in his view about the nature of the *moral* duty of democratic governments in the field of foreign policy. I became fully conscious of that when I read his statement that, in 1941, the Western powers should not have entered a military alliance with Stalin because "world democracy could have defeated one totalitarian regime after another, the German, then the Soviet." Leaving aside the utter unreality of that "alternative," I want to stress its moral implication: in Solzhenitsyn's view, to engage in war against Soviet totalitarianism was as much the moral duty of the West as to fight Nazi totalitarianism, regardless of the fact that Hitler had occupied a number of Western countries and threatened the security of the remainder while Stalin did not. The evil of Stalinist totalitarianism in itself, apart from its international actions (which included the period of active complicity with Hitler's aggressions ended only by Hitler's change of front), would apparently have morally justified a Western war against Russia.

This reasoning is morally unacceptable for any democratic government, for the latter exists primarily to protect the security and welfare of its own people, to whom it is responsible, and who consist no more of heroes and saints than the Russian people consist of Solzhenitsyns. A democratic government is not free to engage in war "to make the world safe for democracy," though democratic governments have repeatedly pretended just that; it is only free, and indeed obliged, to defend democracy in order to assure its own safety.

Defense of that safety does not start only at its borders, but often requires the defense of the security of other, more exposed countries, with whom alliances are concluded for that purpose, and it may suffer gravely if such allies are abandoned under pressure, as Czechoslovakia was abandoned by France under the Munich agreement of 1938. But no democratic government has the right, let alone the duty, to risk the lives of its citizens in a war to overthrow a foreign government, however evil, that does not attack itself or its allies and therefore does not threaten its safety in the sense of a clear and present danger.

Laws of History

I admit that I did not always take that view. When I first came to Britain as a young refugee from Hitler's Germany, I thought of the early efforts of the Western powers to find terms of "coexistence" with Hitler's regime as immoral because of the evil nature of nazism. Today, I think that these efforts were merely shortsighted and mistaken because the Western governments did not realize that Hitler did not only want to increase his power, but actually wanted war because of his commitment to achieving total victory within a short time. Stalin did not want world war, nor do his successors— they believe that the "laws of history" will enable them to get all they want without risking all they have gotten. That is reason enough to resist their expansion, even at a risk; it is no reason to regard total war with them as inevitable, and it was no reason for that even in Stalin's time.

Solzhenitsyn reproaches the West: "At the first threat of Hitlerism you stretched out your hands to Stalin." In fact, France negotiated an alliance with Stalin in 1935, but never implemented it by a concrete military agreement because Stalin demanded the right to march, in case of war, through Poland and Romania, both allied with France, and they refused. After the Munich agreement, even the paper alliance was dead. Britain began to discuss an alliance with Russia in 1939 not "at the first threat of Hitlerism," but after Hitler had broken the Munich agreement and taken all Czechoslovakia by force. This time the negotiations failed because the British would not grant to Stalin the right to march, in case of war with Germany, through the Baltic states—and Stalin preferred a pact with Hitler who had no such qualms.

The real "stretching out of hands" occurred in 1941 when Hitler invaded Russia. Solzhenitsyn may not remember it, but what he calls "Hitler's little Germany" had by then occupied continental Europe from the Atlantic to the Russian frontier, and Britain alone was left fighting him, with the sympathy and economic backing of a militarily uncommitted United States. Solzhenitsyn tells us, after more than thirty years, that Britain in her deadly peril, and the United States concerned with Britain's survival, should have refused to encourage and aid Russia's resistance and thus divide Hitler's forces for as long as possible. This might well have enabled Hitler to force a "Brest-Litovsk peace" on Stalin first and then turn back against Britain with all Europe's resources at his command while Japan engaged the United States!

"England, France, the United States were victorious in the Second World War," writes Solzhenitsyn. "Victorious states always dictate peace, they receive firm conditions . . . . Instead of this, beginning in Yalta, your statesmen of the West, for some inexplicable reason, have signed one capitulation after another." The victorious states did indeed dictate their conditions, but they included the Soviet Union, which had not only borne a great part of the burden and sacrifice of the war, but had advanced its armies to the heart of Europe in the process; when Captain Solzhenitsyn was arrested around the time of Yalta, his unit stood on Prussian soil. The West could not have removed the Soviets from the conquered lands against their will without war—either then or since. Solzhenitsyn speaks movingly of his hopes of meeting the American soldiers at the Elbe. Does he really think the Western powers, at that moment, should or could have turned their arms against the Russian forces, who had defeated Hitler together with them, for another war? But if that was excluded, a compromise giving Stalin the chance to maintain control of Eastern Europe, which Russia had won by her part in destroying Hitler's empire, was inevitable.

It is true that the compromise was made worse than it need have been by President Roosevelt's illusions about the nature and aims of Stalin's regime; that the Western forces could have advanced farther in the last weeks of the war, as Churchill vainly proposed, which would have created a better basis for postwar negotiations; and that the infamous surrender of unwilling Soviet citizens for "repatriation" (in which American as well as British forces took part) could have been avoided. But it was inevitable that the Western powers' capacity to determine the future of Europe ended more or less where it ends today—at the military demarcation line reached at the end of the fighting.

There follows a period about which Solzhenitsyn is, for once, inconsistent. On one side, he speaks of thirty years of "constant retreat" during which "more was surrendered to totalitarianism than any defeated country has ever surrendered after any war in history." That bears no resemblance to the real history of the cold war period. On the other side, he mentions examples of successful Western, particularly American, firmness from that period—breaking the Berlin blockade by the airlift in 1948, checking aggression in Korea in 1950-1951, forcing a withdrawal of Soviet rockets from Cuba in 1962. These were not isolated exceptions, in a general retreat, but critical climaxes in a long drawn-out struggle to resist Soviet expansion by use of threat of force—a struggle conducted under American leadership, albeit not by Americans alone. That struggle was begun by the warnings of the British Labour government's foreign secretary, Ernest Bevin, before the American government decided to take it up; it included the resistance of the people of Berlin to the blockade as well as the Anglo-American airlift; the decision of the West Europeans to cooperate in the joint rebuilding of Europe with the help of the Marshall Plan and the defeat of the Communist strike campaign directed against it; the creation of the North Atlantic Treaty Organization alliance and the growth of its integrated command organization; the united resistance to Khruschev's Berlin ultimatum from 1958-1962, and above all, the entire long struggle to consolidate not only a viable modern economy, but free democratic institutions in Western Europe and Japan that had both been prostrate in 1945.

During the same long period, there were also the kind of internal crises that are inevitable in countries with free institutions, and the kind of quarrels and conflicts between allies that are inseparable from the respect of their national independence. What did not occur was just what Solzhenitsyn writes about—constant retreat and capitulation. Nor was there, as Solzhenitsyn writes, only a generous America that "sometimes" resisted while the Europeans merely "counted their nickels," relied on American protection and had "even less will to defend themselves than South Vietnam": one wonders who has given Solzhenitsyn, who has never lived in Western Europe and has had neither time nor need to study the postwar history of Europe or even the defense budgets of the Federal Republic, Britain or France, this sort of slanted picture—or what made him think he would encourage the Americans to firmer resistance against totalitarianism by teaching them to despise their European allies!

Political Stalemate

If the West has been unable to find peaceful methods for "liberating" or aiding in the self-liberation of any country from Soviet-type communism during these thirty years, with the exception of Yugoslavia, the Soviet Union has also been unable to subject a single new country to its regime by use or threat of force. That is not a story of constant retreat and capitulation, but of a stalemate maintained by bitter political struggle.

What then does Solzhenitsyn's picture of thirty years of shame rest on? It clearly rests on the fact that during this period China came under Communist rule in 1949, Cuba in 1959-1961 and Vietnam and the rest of Indochina in stages since 1954. That is a series of tragedies for the people concerned, but it did not come about in any one of these cases by Western surrender to Soviet power and pressure. Rather, while Soviet expansion was successfully contained at considerable risk, cost and effort, those countries fell to Communist-led revolutionary uprisings (or in Cuba, to the Communist transformation of an originally non-Communist revolutionary movement). Though the Soviet leaders welcomed these Communist victories, they were due not to Soviet strength, but to independent developments in the countries concerned. Soviet intervention played no major role in the Communist victory in China, and Western intervention could not have prevented it—just as more Western intervention could not have prevented the Bolshevik victory in Russia (or does Solzhenitsyn believe that this was also due to a "surrender" by the West?).

Soviet aid became important for Cuba only after Castro was firmly in power and chose to align himself with Russia. During the several phases of the thirty years' war in Vietnam, Soviet military aid to the Communists was indeed substantial, but no more so than American aid first to the French and later to South Vietnam; and no Soviet (or Chinese) troops marched in to fight the American troops after 1965. What happened there was not a Western surrender, but a defeat of the weaker and less coherent anti-Communist forces of the

South by the combined forces of the Communists from North and South Vietnam, despite years of direct and massive American intervention—a defeat whose ultimate inevitability was apparent to critical observers even before that intervention began.

Dual Nature

What is at issue here—and what Solzhenitsyn has not yet understood—is the inescapable dual nature of the struggle against the spread of Communist totalitarianism. On one hand, it requires containment of expansion of one or more Communist powers by the determined and skillful use of Western power. That is the side Solzhenitsyn sees, even if he oversimplifies it. On the other hand, it requires a political competition with independent, native Communist movements in widely varying and often extremely unfavorable conditions, above all in a number of underdeveloped countries. That is the aspect he has so far failed to take into account. The outcome of this competition ultimately depends on the attractiveness and cohesion of the native opponents of totalitarianism. In some important cases, the defeat of those has proved inevitable, but it had nothing to do with a Western surrender. It has thus far been matched by the defeat of all Communist bids for power in advanced industrial countries.

While the disastrous end of the Vietnam War was a tragedy for the Vietnamese people and a defeat for the United States and hence for the West, it was not a victory achieved by the Soviet Union. The American withdrawal was not undertaken because of Soviet threats or to please the Soviet Union— witness the mining of the Vietnamese harbors at the time of President Nixon's visit to Moscow in 1972. Because of that, it is also wrong to use Vietnam as a yardstick to measure the value of détente. What happened there was neither the result of a sham détente, nor could it have been prevented by a successful détente. The outcome in Vietnam did not decisively depend on the state of relations between the superpowers, while the concept of détente refers, in the main, to those relations.

That brings us to the present and the future. Whatever Solzhenitsyn may think about 1941 and 1945, he certainly does not want a war between the West and the Soviets now, as he realizes it would be a nuclear holocaust. Because of that, he agrees that détente is "as necessary as air—it's the only way of saving the earth." But it must be "true détente [based] not on smiles, not on verbal concessions [but] on a firm foundation." To be firmly based and reliable, such a "true détente" must have three main characteristics: the end not only of the use of war, but of the violence used by the Soviet regime to oppress its dissident countrymen; the subjection of that regime to the control of a free public opinion and a freely elected parliament, which alone would prevent it from breaking any international agreement "overnight", and the end of Communist "ideological warfare."

These three "simple" conditions for détente clearly amount to one even simpler thing: the end of Communist one-party rule in Russia. The wish for the end of Communist ideological warfare and of the persecution of Soviet dissidents, for a free press and free elections in Russia will certainly be shared by the immense majority of Westerners (though Solzhenitsyn himself only recently expressed grave doubts about the desirability of a parliamentary democracy for his country). But Solzhenitsyn, for all the sincerity of his prophecy, is not a fool; he clearly does not expect such a radical transformation of the Soviet regime to come about by the struggle of his fellow dissidents in the foreseeable future. Can he possibly believe that the West could bring it about by making it a condition for any kind of détente?

He must know that if we demand the abdication of the Soviet Communist party from power as the price of détente, it will refuse: even Lenin accepted the ultimatum of Brest-Litovsk only in order to retain power, and the relation of forces between the two superpowers and their blocs today is one of approximate equals, not like that between victorious imperial Germany and defeated Russia in 1917. A "true détente," as defined by Solzhenitsyn, is thus strictly unobtainable under present conditions. What is his alternative if nuclear war is to be excluded?

We can glimpse the answer from Solzhenitsyn's statement that even before the military alliance of 1941, the American recognition of the Soviet government in 1933 was an "unprincipled" deal with totalitarianism. Solzhenitsyn's "principled" alternative to détente with the existing Communist party regime, therefore, is to have no dealings with such a regime at all. Not only no economic trade or cooperation which helps the Communists overcome some of the weaknesses of their system; not only no Conference on European Security which "once and for all signs away Eastern Europe"; but obviously no negotiations on limiting nuclear arms and rocketry either, since in the absence of a free press and parliament, the Soviet leaders would be free to break any agreement "overnight." And logically, not even ordinary diplomatic relations between the superpowers—certainly no attempts at joint crisis management, no "hot wire" to avert catastrophe at critical moments.

In a world divided between two nuclear superpowers—and divided not only by power rivalry, but by a conflict of principles—it would be criminally irresponsible for the democratic superpower to refuse communication with its opponent because of its loathing for the latter's political system, for communication is the only way to control the risk of total destruction to "save the earth." But communication means negotiation of agreements to reduce the risks, to limit armaments, to defuse acute crises—agreements with a government whose principles we reject as it rejects ours. That is the inescapable logic of "peaceful coexistence."

These necessities of survival have been broadly recognized by both sides in the conflict since the summit meeting of 1955, and have gradually led to such agreements as the nuclear test ban and the nonproliferation treaty. Note that these agreements have not been broken by the Soviet Union despite the lack of public control of its leaders because they were so framed as to be in its interest as well as in that of the West. For despite the fundamental conflict, both sides share one common interest—survival.

Common Interest

Détente, as it has developed since about 1969, includes a little more: it is an effort to limit not only the forms of the conflict, but its range—to settle some of the regional issues in dispute. That has proved easier in some parts of the world than in others: in the heart of Europe, including the city of Berlin from which I write, the fact that American and Soviet forces have been confronting each other along fixed lines for so long has made it possible at last to come to a formal agreement that neither side will violate the status quo by force. The European conference which Solzhenitsyn describes as the "funeral of Eastern Europe" has added nothing to this principle of renunciation of external violence, except that it has phrased it in such a way that the wording would apply also to violence among Communist-ruled states—of the type of Soviet intervention in Hungary in 1956 and Czechoslovakia in 1968.

If Solzhenitsyn believes that by signing the conference documents, Western Europe (and the United States!) has declared "that it is perfectly willing to see Eastern Europe be crushed and overwhelmed once and for all," he should ask the Yugoslavs and Romanians about it. While the impact of that document is, in a limited way, positive for the future of

Eastern Europe, I agree with Solzhenitsyn that, in this case, there is little guarantee for the positive elements.

On the whole, while the need to control the risks and therefore the forms of the East-West conflict is basic and constant for both sides, the prospects of détente in the sense of the search for regional settlements of parts of the conflict are more uncertain, depending both on local developments (in the Middle East, for example) and on changes in Soviet political strategy. But for democratic governments, this uncertainty can be no reason to reject any chance to reduce the risk of international violence if it can be obtained without retreat and on the basis of maintaining a balance of strength.

Yet Solzhenitsyn is not alone with his warnings against a sham détente. A number of responsible Western critics have lately raised their voices in a similar direction. While I disagree with some of their objections against the agreements that have actually been concluded, I sympathize with their concern at the public mood that accompanied these developments in some Western countries for a certain period—at the illusion that settlement of some partial conflict would herald a disappearance of the overall conflict of systems. While no Western government has fully shared these illusions, it is worth recalling that in the spring of 1973, a few months before the most recent Middle East war, a presidential message to Congress advanced the doctrine that a point had been reached in East-West rivalry where neither side could gain political advantage from further marginal increases of power. As could have been foreseen and as events have shown, that optimistic doctrine was wrong.

It is in the conviction that the conflict is not going to disappear (because it is a conflict between systems founded on opposite principles as well as a rivalry between two superpowers) that I agree with Solzhenitsyn. Here the political value of his warnings emerges—in enlightening Western opinion on the nature of Soviet official ideology and on the

human consequences of the system of government based on
it. It is Western opinion, rather than Western governments,
that has often helped the victims of that system and can help
them more by drawing attention to their fate and showing the
Soviet government that it is not indifferent to the inhuman
persecution of those who stand up for human rights. The
Western governments cannot make the ending of that persecution a condition for agreements with the Soviets because
the Soviets will not change the methods of their internal
system under the pressure of foreign governments, and because those agreements are not only in the Soviet, but also in
the Western interest—in the interests of peace. But Western
opinion—parties and the press, trade unions and businessmen, writers and scholars—can make the Soviet leaders
aware of how much they have to lose by inhuman actions.

Solzhenitsyn's true and important message should be addressed to that Western opinion wherein he is universally
respected. It is by being wrongly addressed to Western governments, that have the duty to follow other considerations,
that it became for once a wrong message.

Solzhenitsyn as Pseudo-Moralist

Norman Birnbaum

A Manichean world view typically arises in times when all values end. The striking thing about Solzhenitsyn's attempt to interpret world politics in Manichean terms is that it purports to rest on an intact set of beliefs—in pluralism, representative democracy and civil liberties. Solzhenitsyn finds a sort of secular perfection in Western institutions, particularly in those of the United States. His Manichean conflict opposes perfected good to (no less perfected) evil, as embodied in Soviet state and society. Rather than postulating the coming of a cosmic conflict which would annihilate inauthentic forms of existence, Solzhenitsyn thinks that we are in that conflict now. His Manicheanism is ahistorical; it is pseudo-Manichean because of its invented, artificial quality.

It is invented in another sense. In Solzhenitsyn's other writings, he appears less convinced of the ultimate validity of the values he affects to espouse. His prescriptions for an end to the Soviet regime take us back to a Russian ideology remote from liberalism. Indeed, many of the abhorrent features of the Soviet regime stem from its historical continuity with the czarist state. Worse, however, is the antihistorical quality of Solzhenitsyn's position. He ignores the real conflicts of world politics, the effective constraints on nations, the content of the recent past and of the present. Were he to

121

ask for a new beginning, an apocalyptic view might have a certain justification in the insufficiencies and horrors of our epoch. But what he asks for is something else: that we take at face value the kind of political ideology even our present leaders (monsters of ineptitude, hypocrisy and lust for power) would be ashamed to promulgate.

Policy of Coexistence

The Soviet Union's regime is so repellent that our own political institutions seem (and are) benign by comparison. That, however, is not the point Solzhenitsyn makes. He argues that we are lending support to the regime by the policy (or policies, since there are several varieties, all of which he confounds) of coexistence. Has it occurred to Solzhenitsyn that the Nixon-Ford-Kissinger policy of coexistence is entirely connected to Kissinger's role as the foreign minister of large-scale capitalism in America, a role exemplified in his many years on Nelson Rockefeller's private payroll? Coexistence is, at present, good for business. The combination of coexistence and maintenance of the arms race is good for two sorts of business: arms production for the home market (and for a certain amount of export) and capital deals with the Soviet Union. That the policy has been worked out with the Soviet ruling class makes it more, not less, attractive to our own; rather than dealing with the vagaries of a liberated Soviet public opinion or with a Soviet leadership actually committed to socialist revolution, our own moral pygmies confront theirs. If this analysis of the kind of coexistence we now have is correct, then what of the liberal substance of society, upon which Solzhenitsyn would draw for a confrontation with the Soviet system? Our own substance is, in fact, attenuated.

It is easy enough to see that Solzhenitsyn exaggerates, or more aptly, caricatures our world political position. Eastern Europe could have been wrenched from the Soviet armed forces only by beginning a third world war as the second ended. A heightening of confrontation now would increase the risks (already far too large) of a thermonuclear conflict and with it, of the destruction of every semblance of civilization on the globe—as well as unspeakable suffering for hundreds of millions. It is unnecessary to become fulsome about Ford and Brezhnev to the point of saying that they are not totally devoid of sense; a thermonuclear war would be the ultimate human catastrophe.

Solzhenitsyn has ignored another point. Our own experience of the cold war is that it did much to corrode, even undermine, the kind of liberalism in whose name he would revive it. This was a climate in which social experimentation was difficult, if not impossible; in which our own civil liberties were threatened by the Federal Bureau of Investigation and the Central Intelligence Agency (as well as by a manufactured popular cretinism) and intervention in the affairs of many other countries—even to the extent of corrupting our cultural life by the development of anticommunism as a very large and profitable intellectual racket.

Moral Pathos

It would be irresponsible to advance these arguments without acknowledging the moral pathos of some of Solzhenitsyn's argument. We should not be passive spectators to the persecution of intellectuals, the denial of rights of emigration and the institutionalised obscurantism of the Soviet regime. Given the world political limits of our situation, what can be done? One solution would incorporate long- and short-term components. The long-term element is simple enough—and intolerably difficult. The construction of a good society in this country and the development of forms of pluralistic and democratic socialism in more politically advanced areas (above all Western Europe) may create tensions in Soviet politics and society which can be resolved only by liberalization. It is by no means certain that they would do so. The present Soviet leadership has shown ample skepticism about Italian communism's revisionism, and supported D'Estaing against the Union de Gauche in the 1974 elections in France; it is not enthusiastic about libertarian socialism. A Western Europe well along that path might encourage more, rather than less, repression in the Soviet Union, for fear of ideological contagion. Perhpas the Eastern European nations can serve as areas of conduction, although the Czech case shows the limits of that. In any event, no other long-term strategy seems worthwhile.

A short-term strategy would devolve upon the citizenry as well as the governments of Western nations. Nothing in the imprecise rules of coexistence prevents protest against specific Soviet domestic acts. In particular, Soviet intellectuals have shown their awareness of foreign protest and pressures. Solzhenitsyn would have us believe that the Soviet intelligentsia is totally powerless to deal with its regime, but that does not appear to be the case. In brief, it may be possible to develop many of the immediate forms of pressure without resorting to a catastrophic perspective.

Finally, what about the Soviet dissidents, the Soviet opposition? What is disheartening about Solzhenitsyn's speech is the way in which he writes the opposition off. It is not for those of us who live under the Bill of Rights to give lessons to those who live under the Soviet Constitution. Without a large-scale movement of protest within the Soviet Union, however, it is difficult to see how that society can be changed.

An Amnesty
International of One

Irving Louis Horowitz

The only meaningful comparison that one can make to the impact of Solzhenitsyn's speeches during his recent visit to the United States is Winston Churchill's famous "Iron Curtain" speech in Fulton, Missouri, in 1947, in which he formally declared the beginning of the cold war. While the Churchillian event was conducted, quite properly, in an abbey, under the most austere, collegiate auspices in the American Midwest, Solzhenitsyn's speech, under the sponsorship of the American Federation of Labor and Congress of Industrial Organizations (AFL-CIO), represented an almost typical Washington happening. As a study in contrasts, it would be hard to improve upon the introductory remarks of George Meany, with his carefree working-class mannerisms straight out of Casey Stengel, and Solzhenitsyn's classical nineteenth-century Russian oratory. One is tempted to declare: "Only in America!"

Solzhenitsyn's opening speech in Washington, on June 30, 1975, can only be described as a cross between a Southern Baptist Convention and a chapter from television's "This Is Your Life." Solzhenitsyn was introduced to people (some from his past) who have also managed to escape the ferocious world of Soviet terrorism—a sailor who had jumped ship, was returned and finally was permitted to leave under United States pressure, and a United States citizen who spent a number of years in the Gulag and is now a government employee, Alexandr Dolgun. These people were brought together not so much because of shared interests, but because they had shared perils. The ceremonialism of the occasion was marked by the presence of a bishop of the Russian Orthodox Church, who offered the invocation and benediction, and several secular bishops and dignitaries, past and present, from the United States government, such as Daniel Patrick Moynihan, William Rogers, Melvin Laird and James R. Schlesinger. It was Kremlinology in reverse. Seating assignments became important to establish the hierarchy of power present, and one gossiped over the absence of Kissinger, as much as over the appearance of Schlesinger.

All of this background paraphernalia was neither unimportant nor incidental. With remarkable agility, Solzhenitsyn has become an American politician *manquée*, traveling the length and breadth of the country, pumping hands, kissing babies and assuming a reverential stance before the proper monuments. He is sufficiently "Westernized" to know that sponsorship is legitimacy. The vocation of orator is not a universe of Wittgenstein's making, i.e., whereof one does not know, thereof one does not speak. Rather, whatever one knows, be sure it gets listened to. That Solzhenitsyn did quite brilliantly and adroitly, by having his premiere effort sponsored by the AFL-CIO national office. It is, after all, the central organization of the American working class, and hence it is an organization whose roots touch the fabric of American life, and presumably is unlikely to be called reactionary in its essence. That, as much as what Solzhenitsyn said, must have upset President Gerald Ford and Henry Kissinger; both of them have enough trouble with organized labor and a disorganized Congress.

Fusion of Sentiments

Solzhenitsyn somehow fused and organized a welter of critical sentiments and feelings that most ordinary Americans still retain toward the Soviet government. The cold war may be over and spaceship diplomacy may be the next step toward political paradise, but still there is that undigested residue of mistrust, with thirty years standing. There are differences between us and them, between Americans and Russians, and even more, between democrats and communists. Solzhenitsyn tapped that sentiment, and understood how to fuse it and how to use it to develop a broad coalition. His speech revealed a high level of sophistication. He employed the organizing symbols and myths of American political life, extending from the anti-bourgeois spirit to pro-democratic sentiment.

One must consider that President Ford's Helsinki trip would have been just one more stop on a European itinerary if Solzhenitsyn had not raised the SOS and pointed out that Helsinki is what the European trip was all about. Helsinki, he remarked, represented the final solution of World War II, the absolute crystallization of a divided Europe, the transformation of the Iron Curtain into a Steel Girder. Only then were Ford and Kissinger compelled to change the rhetoric, if not the reality, of the situation. The fact is that the Helsinki agreement was viewed by the President of the United States as a new opportunity for humanitarianism, and by the Premier of the Soviet Union as a final termination of all Western interference in East European affairs. The agreement settled very little, but that is not the point. The point is that a writer, Solzhenitsyn, became, albeit briefly, a counterforce to Kissinger in American political life. In rocking the policy consensus, the foreigner and exiled dreamer, Solzhenitsyn, had the weight of American tradition on his side.

A great deal has been said, and much has been made of Solzhenitsyn's religious mysticism and pan-Slavism. If these elements exist (they have been reflected in his literary works), they are not the paramount concerns of Solzhenitsyn the political figure. There is nothing mystical or theological about his political sentiments. He reveals himself to be an old-fashioned Western liberal, a believer in democratic pluralism and laissez-faire individualism. In part, his position derives from his role as a writer in Western exile. In part, too, it derives from a clear decision to assume a posture to the political right of the dissidents who remain in the Soviet Union, such as Roy Medevev and the other *Samizdatists*. In short, there is a tactical consideration involved. By reintroducing fundamental concerns, Solzhenitsyn has created an opening, not only for authentic dialogue, but for more moderately toned criticisms to be treated with greater respect and realism within the Soviet Union.

Political Potency

Solzhenitsyn is a remarkable figure, possessing a political potency not found since Trotsky. Not only was he permitted to emigrate from the Soviet Union with family and library intact, but the West treated him as a celebrity (quite unlike Trotsky). Solzhenitsyn's responsibilities to Russian politics remain central, even in exile. Even more unusual, he is not a Communist party member in opposition like Sakharov. We are presented with a living Russian anti-Communist who sees value, not in the interior Marxist "dialogue," but only in the dialogue between autocracy and democracy. The drama itself is indicative of new times: the Soviet Union, whatever its social structure, now has the capacity and the confidence to permit exile as a solution rather than death, and, equally, the United States is in the odd position of having this lonely exile serve as the organizing principle of opposition to détente, and, for that matter, a focus of animosity for upsetting delicate diplomatic equilibrium.

The Washington speech was in part a brief history of the Communist party in the Soviet Union. It surveys the ways in which the Soviet Union has been propped up by the United States and Western Europe during its nearly sixty-year history. It is a call to moral arms demanding a *quid pro quo* in the way of human rights for economics and political concessions. Solzhenitsyn clearly feels the United States has never gotten any bargaining advantages from its recognition of the Soviet regime to the present. There is a strange manichaeanism about Solzhenitsyn's presentation: the United States is represented as naive while the Soviet Union is represented as cunning. It provides a counterrevisionist reading of history with respect to the origins of the cold war. For while the revisionist historians have been busy working out the ways in which the postwar Truman administration undermined the World War II alliance, Solzhenitsyn shows how the prewar Roosevelt administration may be characterized by its genteel capitulation to Soviet terrorism as well as Soviet expansionism.

Anyone acquainted with *Mission to Moscow* and the whitewash of the Soviet Purge Trials surely cannot scoff at such an approach. If Truman was suspicious of Soviet postwar intentions, Roosevelt was ingenuous with regard to Soviet prewar performance. From Finland, to the Baltic States, to Bessarabia, the United States acquiesced in geographic and demographic changes of a sweeping order. The "booty of war" overwhelmed the "rights of man."

Solzhenitsyn does not oppose détente, which he considers to be "as necessary as air." What he perceives in the present moment is not East-West détente but Western capitulation. World War III is being won by Soviet diplomats without firing a shot. Indeed, what is one to make of the constant Marxist claims that imperialism is shrinking, that the United States is collapsing, that the forces of socialism are expanding, that the forces of communism are inevitable and victorious? Is this not simply the other side of Solzhenitsyn's claims—spoken in an optative rather than pessimistic mood?

We are partially involved in empirical questions. What, in fact, is occurring on a worldwide scale with respect to global politics? Is the United States losing and the Soviet Union winning? Are the forces of imperialism shrinking while the forces of communism are enlarging? Here is where Solzhenitsyn seems to have his greatest difficulties. Because in some measure, whether he would care to admit it or otherwise, he is employing the intellectual coin of the realm of Spengler and the *Decline of the West*. The theme of creeping barbarism is the linchpin which, if pulled, collapses the argument and would compel the dialogue to become more realistic and sober on both sides.

American and Russian Realities

In economic terms, capitalism had a period of "longwave" growth between 1945 and 1973 (the so-called *Kondratieff* effect) that not even its most severe critics seriously challenge. The emergence of new forms of production, distribution and organization, labeled multinationalism, has not only "rationalized" capitalist relations by internationalizing them, but further, created a mechanism for dealing with multinational socialism. We are at a point where no pure theory of capitalism or socialism can be sustained because no pure example of either system exists. Bureaucratic centralization, mass social welfare services and state allocation and manipulation of the economic system typify both American and Russian realities. The United States and the Soviet Union may not be converging, but certainly there are parallels between their economic systems that make détente functionally as well as strategically plausible—if not downright inevitable.

Overall characterizations are inevitably impressionistic and subject to modification. What seems to be taking place is not so much the demise of capitalism or the creeping triumph of bolshevism, but a trade-off reaching toward an equilibrium point. Solzhenitsyn is correct to note the considerable triumph of the Soviet Union in Eastern Europe and Southeast Asia. But it is likewise the case that the United States has also expanded, rather than contracted, its sphere of influence since the end of World War II. In both political and military terms, American hegemony has been extended to include vast stretches of Latin America, Africa and Asia. Even the Arab Middle East is shaping up as a new player in the capitalist orbit. Hence, while the political forms of Third World nations are often highly centralized, totalitarian and overtly military, their economic forms remain quite clearly entrenched in the capitalist world system. The trade-off is thus not simply on a nation-for-nation basis, but also gives sway to communism or totalitarianism in the political network and increasing capitalist control in the economic sector.

This may not be a pleasant outcome to the postwar drama for reconstruction, nor does either option offer much hope in the way of individual freedom. Yet Solzhenitsyn believes, and quite properly, that an enormous gap exists between those nations fully under Soviet dominion and those that still retain a measure of democratic self-determination. The point is that Solzhenitsyn's manicheanism breaks down under the weight of empirical guidelines. The West is neither entirely naive nor blameless, while the East is neither entirely victorious nor immoral. What makes Solzhenitsyn's response especially poignant is the relative absence of moral considerations in the conduct of foreign policy. If the Soviets can readily wear the mask of evil, the United States does not nearly do as well wearing a crown of thorns. For this reason, the morally centered political universe of Solzhenitsyn fails to convince under careful examination.

Solzhenitsyn's charges and claims tend to fall on deaf ears and to be viewed as the ravings of a weird literary romantic because empirical and historical events tend to be viewed as ethically neutral or ambiguous. The time machine has passed him by: one might say for worse rather than for better. But in all ages writers have claimed the prerogative of looking backward as well as looking forward. After all, even the most hard-boiled of us can say that in the Soviet Union we have seen the future and it works, if by "work" we mean stumbling along. Under such circumstances, it is easier to say we have seen the past and it worked even better.

Price of Suffering

Solzhenitsyn, in effect, says that under Czarism there was less terrorism, less imprisonment and less homicide than under Stalinism. But he never quite answers the question of whether Czarism was superior to Stalinism. He cannot quite bring himself to confront the central issue of any revolution: is the price in suffering worth the pain in output? The absolute moralist in him disallows an acceptance of the present Soviet regime; whereas the shrewd historian similarly disallows advocacy of any return to the Czarist regime. Hence, Solzhenitsyn must end in a *cul-de-sac* from which he is incapable of extricating himself.

There is an isomorphism and similitude between the internal workings of the United States and the Soviet Union. From Left to Right there is agreement that this is the case. At the very historical juncture when there seems to be a growing intensity in ideological debates within each major power, there is a noticeable decline in ideological disputations between major world powers. It is simply too risky to undertake armed struggle or its economic equivalencies in a thermonuclear age. Thus ideological debate is taken down one notch to *inner*national levels. Today, all major problems are managed bureaucratically. Political controversies become ambiguous, if not in their nature, then in their solution. From the point of view of the major powers, struggles between Greece and Turkey, Israel and Egypt, Uganda and Tanzania, Flemish and Walloons, are all trivial, dangerous only to the extent that they might conceivably ignite the world in nuclear holocaust.

Big-Power Management

What has happened in recent years to create an elitist reaction to critics of the Soviet regime like Solzhenitsyn? Certainly it has not been any dramatic democratization of the regime. To be sure, a profound curb to internal terrorism has taken place. The very release of Solzhenitsyn indicates as much. But the accusations now leveled by him have been made in the past by a range of authorities from Boris Nicolaevsky concerning Russian slave labor camps and their victims, to Hannah Arendt who in *The Origins of Totalitarian Democracy* rendered an accurate portrait of the Nazi conception of nature and the Bolshevik conception of history as ending in the same swamp of human degradation. I rather suspect that the officialist resentment for Solzhenitsyn is part of the American experience with defeat in military adventures in Southeast Asia and social and economic stalemate domestically. As a consequence, big power chauvinism has become a new style, wrapped in the phraseology of détente. It is a last effort to turn defeat into victory, even if it means sharing the fruits of such success with a much feared Soviet adversary. Along comes Solzhenitsyn to remind us of the chasm between democracy and autocracy and the schism between the twentieth century history of the United States in contrast to the Soviet Union. Now, we somehow hope that by ignoring the past, defeat can still be turned into victory, cold war into détente.

As a result, détente comes down to big-power management of small nations and their affairs. The price of such management is less autonomy for nations and less freedom for individuals. In this connection, Solzhenitsyn cannot easily be confounded. We can say that there are no alternatives or that the risks are too great to steer a different course, but in fact we are in an anomaly. The end of the cold war is bringing relief from the possibility of military destruction, but it has not yet brought in its wake relief from political terror or personal insecurity.

Détente, to the very extent that it is successful, makes politics even more remote; decisions are made on high. Solzhenitsyn is responding to this sense of the present situation. He is, after all, the perfect Orwellian, who understands that history is memory and that injustice, like justice, is indivisible. There can be no justice for a prisoner in the United States without justice for prisoners in the Soviet Union. There can be no terrorism in the Soviet Union without opening up that possibility in the United States. That monistic sense of political events, that feeling that the world is one and that Russians have as much right to speak with candor about the United States as Americans about the Soviet Union, makes Solzhenitsyn a special figure: an Amnesty International of One.